First Flights

Stories of the First Men and Women to Venture Into the Sky

By

Peter C. Conrad

ISBN: 1-4140-4603-0 (e-book)
ISBN: 1-4140-4602-2 (Paperback)

This book is printed on acid free paper.

1stBooks - rev. 12/11/03

Acknowledgements

First Flights would not have been successfully published without the thoughtful comments, encouragement, and professional editing of my wife, Simone.

To
Jessica and Tess

Table of Contents

Preface

Nowadays we look into the clear summer sky to watch a jet mark the distance with its vapor trail without a thought of the time before aircraft. In 1910, men and women lined up along the grass at a summer fair to see a machine that was said to be able to fly. Such claims of miraculous flights were widely doubted. Those people could not be blamed for doubting that flight was possible. The machines were small, resembling kites more than something that could take people into the sky.

Flying was an amazing story of progress and adventure. The tinny kite-like machines that flew at the summer fairs in 1910 and 1911 later led to the heavier flying machines that became weapons during the First World War, flew across the Atlantic, explored the arctic, transported cargo into the high north, and became an important means of travel across North America.

The aircraft had rapidly developed during the First World War. By the 1920s, many looked to the aircraft to solve problems of transportation and communication. Now that an aircraft had made it across the Atlantic, the limits of the machines would be tested in flights over the Rocky Mountains, and into the high north. Vast regions could be surveyed rapidly from the air.

Those who would have been lost in the wilderness could now be rescued. Newspapers reporters could travel rapidly to crime scenes. Gold could be carried from the north by aircraft. In time, airplanes would be able to transport people more rapidly then trains. The aircraft could be effective in tracking down criminals in places where there would have been little chance of finding them.

This book is about the history and spirit of these early flying years. The stories of the experimental flights and the people who flew the machines are an intriguing one.

The stories that follow are based on real events and tell the history of aviation from the point of view of characters invented by the author.

1. The First Biplanes and Pilot School

The story about pioneer pilots and their biplanes begins in a time before airplanes and pilots were common. Even though the Wright brothers had built a flying machine, most people still believed that flying wasn't safe or practical. Pioneer barnstormers began giving flying demonstrations in communities across North America. My name is Charles F. Willard, one of the first of the barnstormers. I flew my biplane at the 1909 summer fair in Toronto, Canada.

I am going to tell you a story about Glenn Curtiss, one of the first to make biplanes for others. Curtiss was also among the first to teach flying; I was his first student. At least, I was as much of a student as I could be. I never had any formal lessons because no one, not even Glenn Curtiss, knew much about flying. When I was chosen to be the first student pilot, I was told that the tiny biplane wasn't big enough for two people. All that could be taught was how to take off and land.

Then, it was up to me to teach myself how to fly. After landing, I asked questions which Glenn tried to answer. We were both students working out the mystery of flight together.

I should tell you how Glenn came to teach flying. It began in 1908 when the American Aeronautic Society decided that flying should be more than experimentation. Flying was to be a demonstration sport. The Society was a group of well to do New Yorkers who united to promote the new phenomena of flying.

It began by trying to persuade a French experimenter to come to New York with his plane to give a demonstration. This failed. The Society then persuaded Glenn to build a biplane and train a pilot for it. To do this, the Aeronautic Society paid Glenn $5,000.

The Society's biplane was delivered July 17, 1909. This first aircraft had the name Curtiss on it. That name became renowned for early biplanes.

The name Glenn gave his biplane was the *Golden Flyer* because it was bright yellow with bright orange struts. It was held together with bamboo and high strand wire cables.

Glenn really built a nice motor. It had four cylinders in a vertical formation and a three-and-a-half inch bore with a four-inch stroke. The motor could go at a top speed of 1300 to 1400 revolutions a minute. The tank held exactly one gallon of gas. That was large enough because flights were short at best in those days.

Another feature of the biplane was that it could be easily assembled and taken apart. This made it possible to put it into packing cases for transporting, which became important later when it was used for touring and doing demonstration flights.

Once the biplane was ready, Glenn Curtiss had to teach me to fly. It didn't take long because there wasn't much to learn. I had to either learn to fly on my own or forget about being a pilot. Curtiss was already a certified pilot with the Aerial Experimental Association. He couldn't just stand on the ground and watch as I took flight after flight. He flew the *Golden Flyer* as much as I did.

After I was trained, Glenn moved quickly to build himself another biplane. While I was touring with the first biplane, Curtiss went to France with a new aircraft. On August 29, 1909, he flew in the first Gordon Bennett Trophy race and won.

I went on to become one of the first barnstorming pilots. The *Golden Flyer* was shipped from New York to Toronto. It was assembled on August 28, 1909 at the amusement park at Scarborough Beach, east of the city.

Well, I couldn't believe it when I arrived in Toronto. The summer fair committee had set aside space between two buildings to set up a tent for the airplane to be placed inside. There was barely enough room outside of the tent to pull the biplane out. The committee must have thought that the airplane would just jump up and take off like a bird. The only place that I could use to take off was in between the two buildings.

The opening between the two buildings faced Lake Ontario. To take off, I had to arrange for a trough of

3

boards to be built to guide the center wheel down. There was only six inches between the ends of the wings on each side and the walls of buildings. In front of me was wide-open water. If I didn't make it into the air, I would land in the lake.

"I'm sure glade it is you that is going to fly this," said Mark, my assistant.

"I think it will be all right," I said.

"I think you're going to end up in the water," he replied. "Should I arrange for a boat to go out and pick you up?"

"That shouldn't be necessary," I said.

"Even if everything is running fine, you could get caught up in that trough."

"We already checked it out. It's fine."

"Let's say you do get into the air, where are you going to land?"

"I guess I'll get a better view from up there. I'll find a place," I said.

"Let's hope it isn't in the lake," he replied.

I was ready to go, but it rained. The flight was delayed until September 2, a cold, cloudy day. Rain threatened again, but it was the end of the fair. I had to go! I felt nervous and little light headed before I was even in the air. I warmed up the motor, let it roar, and then gave the final signal to Mark to let go. The craft rushed down the trough set for it. I stared at the breakwater as I went. The plane took to the air, but it was going too slow. The motor simply was not going as fast as it should. I was flat out over the water and I needed speed to climb. The aircraft was too low to even turn around. I decided to use the height I had to

4

gain speed so that I could pull up, and then turn. I pushed the nose down to speed up. It didn't work because the plane didn't get enough speed on the drop. The motor didn't have the power I hoped it would. Down I went until the inevitable happened; I was in the water about three hundred feet out. The water was cold, but shallow. I stood up and waited to be rescued. The aircraft, which landed with its wheels down and tail high up in the air, was not damaged.

The *Toronto Star* called the flight the grand finale of the summer fair. It was the finale, but it certainly was not grand!

2. Hamilton's Aerial Clipper

I was young back in the summer of 1910. It was the first summer that I was employed at the Minoru Park racetrack. If you don't know, that was on Lulu Island near Vancouver, British Columbia. My job was to clean up after the races and to do odd jobs. Those were some good days. I have an image of myself in ankle high black shoes, knickers, a plaid shirt, and a tweed cap; just like the touring automobile drivers wore. People began to believe anything was possible. Machines were the way of the future! More important to me was the newest invention of them all: the biplane. That summer was the first time I ever saw one and the first time people in my neighborhood saw one.

The flying machine that arrived that spring was piloted by one of those early pioneers of the sky who built their own plane then flew them at the summer fairs. The pilot was Charles Hamilton from California. From what I was told, he built his biplane in the fall of

7

1909. It was ready to fly only four months before he arrived on March 25, 1910. I still find it hard to believe that he learned how to fly the machine that fast.

We were the first group he ever flew for. There was a real good-sized crowd, about 3,500 people, at the park. He flew in over top of the racetrack and circled around. We had been told that men were flying like this down East and in the States, but we couldn't believe what we were seeing. The biplane came closer and closer. We could see the rigging of the wings and hear the roar of the motor. The machine looked like a huge kite, but it was big enough to carry a large motor and a man!

When he came in to land the airplane, it touched the ground and with just a little bit of space came to a stop. It didn't need a long runway like planes do now. I walked to where the machine was as it came to a halt. Even though Charles Hamilton was a small man, I couldn't believe that the biplane in front of me was able to carry him into the air. Hamilton was wearing heavy tweed trousers and a heavy coat with a sweater. I could see his light frame shivering from the cold.

"How do you do? I'm Charles Hamilton," he said as he stepped out of the biplane.

"Hello, I'm Tom. Can I get you anything?"

"No, that's fine," he said. He walked away as though nothing out of the ordinary had occurred.

The machine had an engine behind the wing. It was a biplane with cloth-covered wings and an open body construction.

Later in the day, Hamilton returned to the airplane to fly again. We watched as the motor roared and the biplane skipped along the grass. In a moment, he was flying around the racetrack. I stopped staring up when I heard the sound of a car on the track. The driver was speeding along right under the biplane. He was racing! The car soon gained on the biplane above, speeding up until it was in the lead. Hamilton hadn't noticed because he was watching where he was going, not looking down. He swung wide over the track. If he wanted to win a race, he would have tried to turn tight on the bends in the track like the car. The biplane landed and the pilot stepped down from his seat.

"You lost the race!" I called.

"What race?" replied Hamilton.

"The car on the track was racing you."

"Oh? I wondered what that crazy guy was doing?"

"Do you think you could have won?"

"Maybe if I tried." said Hamilton.

The next day, the local newspaper, the Vancouver's *Daily Province*, had a photograph and a story entitled: "Hamilton's Aerial Clipper." The story was a good description of the day's flying. Yet, there was more to come. The next day Hamilton took his biplane into the air three times.

When Hamilton was in the air, he went north along the Fraser Valley for twenty miles. He was gone for some time. The crowd was beginning to worry as time past. Then, he reappeared. He had set a record for the longest cross-country trip in Canada.

Hamilton's return was recorded in the *Daily Province*: "Everyone crowded about him, asking where he had been. 'New Westminster,' came the reply. Mr. Hamilton, shaking with cold, was immediately supplied with a stimulant. … He described how he had followed the winding course of the North Arm of the river, mounting to 2,500 feet. Then because the temperature was too chilly, he had descended to a lower altitude, which he maintained until he reached New Westminster, where he sank to within nearly 100 feet of the ground. He arrival there caused considerable interest. The streetcars stopped while the occupants watched his revolution. Turning just west of the bridge, he began his homeward flight."

Hamilton's last day in Vancouver was March 28th, a cold day with westerly winds. In spite of the cold, Hamilton was going to go up. Many pilots would never consider flying on a cold day like that.

Hamilton had accepted a challenge to a race. This time, the race was against a horse ridden by Curly Lewis. Hamilton allowed the horse a head start, three-eighths of the mile-long track. As it turned out, the head start was a little too much. The horse won the race by a few feet.

To give us a real show, Hamilton flew his biplane to a great height and then cut the motor. He glided back to the ground with a steep dive and flattened out just in time to make a safe landing. That really proved Hamilton as a master flyer.

Unlike most of the early flyers, Hamilton died only two years later from pneumonia. Most of the other pioneer pilots died when their biplanes crashed.

3. St. Henry on the Prairies

My name is St. Henry, Bob St. Henry. Well okay, my name was not really St. Henry. Before I was well known as a pilot, I was an actor. I used St. Henry as a stage name. When I began flying, I kept it. The only change I made to that name was in 1911 when I was called "Lucky Bob" in Saskatoon, Saskatchewan. I liked that name so much that I used it after my trip.

I had no interest in building my own biplane. Unlike many others in aviation, I had no interest in the details of the flying machine. I was more interested in flying it. Being an actor had something to do with my interest in flying. I wanted to be up there in front of a crowd putting on a show, a one-man circus.

The Curtiss Company built the biplane I brought to Saskatoon. It had a small forty horsepower engine. If the size of engine was good enough for the Curtiss Company, it was good enough for me. Except, as I found out in Saskatoon, I needed more power. I also

11

needed to know more about flying if I was going to fly in many summer fairs.

I thought that the prairie would be the simplest place in the world to fly. There were few hills and not much else to run into. The weather couldn't be a problem. There was nothing but sunny skies. Was I wrong!

I arrived at the annual fair in Saskatoon on May 17, 1911. The high winds kept me on the ground for two days. On May 19, I decided to fly no matter how bad the wind was. I started the biplane down the grass, then let the motor have all the gas it could take. With a real effort, I barely got off the ground. The biplane labored upward. I could see that I might be in a little trouble. I was about sixty feet in the air when a gust of wind hit the front end. The front of the biplane shot up. I felt like I was standing still in mid-air. For a moment I felt like I was a kid tumbling on a mat. I was slightly dizzy. I couldn't do anything. The biplane nose-dived straight down! I can barely remember the crash. The people who were nearby helped pull me from the wreckage of the biplane.

As I was lying in the hotel room that night, I thought my flying days were over. I was tired and in pain. When I woke up and saw the bright light of the sun entering my room, I felt great. I couldn't believe that I had been in the crash the day before. I slipped out of bed and resolved that my flying career was not over. The people of Saskatoon had not seen the end of me that year.

I made my way downstairs and sat at a table in the cafe. In minutes Ted, the organizer of the fair, sat down at my table.

"Bob, I am surprised to see you. How do you feel today?"

"I couldn't feel better."

"After that crash yesterday? How could that be? I was sure that was the end of you."

"Oh, come on Ted. Us pilots are a tough bunch. As a matter of fact I am going to keep flying."

"Next summer?"

"This summer. I am going to order a larger engine. I figure I will order a seventy horse-power engine and install it right here in Saskatoon."

"You intend to fly here again this summer?"

"Before the month is over."

"That will be something. Everyone will be glad to see you do it."

"They will see me do it."

It only took a little while to order the engine. My mechanic, Ron, was ready to help with repairs, but he couldn't believe it when I told him I had ordered an eight-cylinder seventy horsepower engine.

"How are we going to mount that motor in the biplane?" he asked.

I must admit I was surprised by the size of the engine when I saw it for the first time.

"Well, what do you think is most important in mounting a motor in a biplane?" I asked.

"I guess it would have to be balance," said Ron.

"How would you figure out the correct balance in this machine?"

13

"I don't know," said Ron as he walked around the biplane.

"You must have some idea."

"We would have to suspend it with the old motor in it and see where it is balanced. I think we could put it on boards to do that."

That is what we did. The biplane was placed on boards that rocked this way and that. We moved the boards up the biplane until we found where the plane was balanced. We marked the position. Then we took the old engine off and placed the new heavier motor in the balanced position. It worked!

I was ready for my first test flight on the evening of June 2nd. I took the biplane up to a height of 250 feet and circled the field three times. I brought the machine down with a careful landing. The biplane was heavier needed more care in flying and landing. Safely on the ground, I was told that the flight was the first successful flight in Saskatchewan.

On June 3rd, I was ready to show the people of Saskatoon a good flight. Because the event had been widely publicized, the fair grounds were crowded. Toward evening, just as I was about to fly before the crowd, the wind came up. I braced myself to take off with a strong wind blowing. I would soon find out if the bigger engine were worth the trouble. I faced the wind and pushed the throttle forward. I could feel the power of the motor. The biplane roared down the field and lifted into the air. I pulled the biplane higher and higher. The wind and the new motor gave me a feeling of more power than I ever had before while I was flying. Soon, I was five hundred feet in the air.

Looking down at the people, I felt satisfied; I had made it. I decided to stay up as long as I could. Around and around I flew. Looking at the wide-open prairie, I felt free. There was plenty of space to fly over.

Finally, I spiraled down and prepared to land. I didn't think I had to be as careful as I had been the day before. I quickly descended to the field. I bounced and then the biplane collapsed to the ground. I skidded to a stop much faster than I had expected. The landing gear under me was crushed. I had to fix that, but I didn't care. I had given the people of Saskatoon a good show!

After that, I went to the United States, but I returned to Regina to fly at the local Dominion fair in August.

My first flight in Regina took place in the evening of August 5th. I took my biplane up for a full six minutes. The crowd was pleased, but that flight was only a start. A little later that evening, I took off again. A huge crowd watched as I flew for seven minutes and showed them some new dips and swoops I had been working on. The crowd watched and gasped as I maneuvered the biplane.

After landing, I decided to go up again. Huge threatening storm clouds hovered in the sky, but there was still a beautiful sunset showing through in the west. There was something magic in the moment. Soon, I was in my biplane racing down the field again. I took to the air, headed westward into the bright sunset toward Government House. The flight was spectacular; it was eight minutes long and I reached a height of 1,200 feet. During the flight, I reached Government House, flew in low, dipped my wings and waved to Lieutenant Governor Brown. Brown clearly returned my salute. When I returned, I was soaked from the rain I had flown through.

The next day, I circled around the Legislature Buildings. I was shocked when I looked down and saw a huge crowd of people waving white serviettes and table clothes from their houses in the residential area. Then on the ninth, I flew for nineteen minutes in high winds and under the threat of rain. I reached a height of 1,600 feet. The crowd was astounded that I flew in such bad conditions. It was a good show. That was all I cared about.

On February 28, 1912, I took the time required to do my test for the Aero Club of America. It was a simple test of circles and a figure eight. I was issued pilot license number one hundred.

4. An Apple for the Judges

My name is Charles. On May 30, 1911, I arrived in Victoria, British Columbia with my Curtiss-Farman biplane to put on a special show. The band of the Fifth Regiment was there to cheer on the crowd.

Early in the day, I was ready to take the machine up. I started the engine and pushed the throttle forward. Soon, I was skipping down the runway. Once my biplane was up in the air, I began to relax and feel as if I was a part of it. The wings were my arms and the power was coming from me, not a motor. I would forget what it felt like to walk. There was just this weightless feeling of floating through the air. For a short time, with the wind hissing by me, I could believe I was a bird. That was the real reason why I wanted to stay in the air for as long as I could. I wanted to see how long I could stay in the air and how far I could go.

When it was time to land, I had to remember who I was and start thinking about how I could bring the aircraft back to the earth I had momentarily forgotten.

My first flight pleased the crowd. I guess that wasn't too hard because only a few, if any, in the crowd had ever seen an airplane fly. All I had to do that summer to please the crowd was get the biplane off the ground. I had been up for more than fifteen minutes at a height of six hundred feet.

I jumped out of the aircraft, relieved that nothing had gone wrong. I didn't want my plane wrecked too soon. I expected to have a few crashes, but I just didn't want them to happen too early in the summer.

The grass was cool and wet as I walked to the fair's concession. It felt good. It was a good day for a baseball game. I loved those summer days when I was a boy. The grass would be cool under my feet. Dad would come into the house and say "How about the ball game?" I knew it would be a great day when that happened. Soon, we would be at the ballpark and the excitement would be all around us. That was what this day was like.

"That was some flying you did sir," said the boy behind the counter.

"Thank you, son."

"What will you have?"

"I guess I will have three of those scones, some lemonade, and maybe, for my next flight, I will have an apple."

"For you next flight?" asked the boy as he put the scones in a paper bag.

"Yeah, sure. This one will be so long that I will need something to eat."

"Do you really think it will be that long a flight?"

"I sure do," I said as I picked up the food. "Make sure you're watching."

"Yes sir."

I ate the scones as I made my way back to the plane. I looked at the apple, and then decided I didn't really want it right away. I pushed it into my pocket. I walked up to the biplane where my engineer, Bob, was working.

"How does the motor look? Is it ready to go up?"

"Yes. The engine is cooled down and the gas tank is full. I say you could have another good flight right now."

"I guess I will be off."

With that, the engine was started. The machine was pointed out at the field. The motor roared and the biplane was rocking down the field. The airplane was not climbing as fast as I had expected. Slowly, it climbed upward. I looked down, relieved to see that I was climbing, but I was still not high enough to clear the trees in front of me. All I could do was dodge them. I successfully rounded several trees. Then, in front of me was a tree that was too high and much wider than any of the others. I turned hard to the right. I heard a loud snapping sound. I had hit a branch. Was the wing ripped? I stared for an unsure moment. No! The branch had broken away and was stuck in my rigging. I felt relieved. The biplane was now just high enough to clear the rest of the trees.

I flew for a few minutes over the trees. Then I circled back to the crowd and looked down at the huge number of people. I felt satisfied and happy. It was like the excitement of going to the ballpark. The air was cool; I felt free and daring. I adjusted my weight in the seat. The apple I had put in my jacket pocket bumped against me. I pulled it out and thought about eating it. After all I deserved it after making my way out of the trees and was putting on a good show. Looking at the bright red color of the apple, a thought struck me.

There was a group of judges down there in the grandstand. Why don't I drop it on them? I thought for a moment. I couldn't remember what they were supposed to be judging, but it didn't matter. I decided not to drop the apple on them. Instead, I would try to fly in as close as I could and throw it at them. I maneuvered the biplane to fly in close, right in front of them. As I was flying close enough to see the faces of the judges, I threw the apple. I missed (and that was probably a good thing), but I did hit the corner of the box they were in.

The next day the local newspaper, the *Victoria Colonist,* reported the event this way, "In traveling past the grandstand he took an apple from his pocket and threw it at the judge's box, striking the corner, which illustrates that the airplane might be destructively useful when employed for military purposes." That sure was the truth, I thought. Oh yes, I kept the branch from the maple tree as a souvenir.

The next day, I flew twice. There were no problems to speak of during that day. The people were satisfied with the demonstration. The community was so happy that on the next day, the school holiday was declared to allow the children to come see me fly.

There were problems with the engine in the morning; all the cylinders were not firing. My mechanic and I worked on the motor into the afternoon. As we were working, a bad gale came up and kept blowing. I couldn't fly even if I wanted to. It was too bad, but there I wasn't going to risk a crash. No way! I wasn't worried about getting hurt, but I didn't want anything to happen to my biplane.

5. Canada's First Post Card Sent by Airplane

I was the postmaster who delivered the first airmail in Canada, not the pilot who flew the airplane. I didn't even know how to fly a biplane that September morning in 1911 when the mail arrived in my post office in the small community of Traynor, Saskatchewan. I must admit, I was really interested in these new flying machines. When I received the postcard that September, I couldn't believe what I read. It was one of the first pieces of mail to be carried on the first flight of airmail in the United Kingdom. The postmaster general of the United Kingdom had issued the card to celebrate the coronation of King George V. There were two halfpenny stamps on the card. On the round cancellation stamp were the words, "First United Kingdom Aerial Post, Sp. 12, 1911, London."

After I retired, I began to research the post card I delivered to Mrs. H.E. Leveson-Gower in 1911. All I could find out was that there was an aerial post card drop only a few weeks before in Quebec City. I really don't think that could be called *mail*.

As the story goes, the French pilot George Mestach had earned his pilot's license from the *Federation Aeronautique Internationale* in France. He arrived in Quebec City on August 30, 1911 and stayed to demonstrate flying until September 5.

He was flying a monoplane called a *Bleriot*. He took his airplane up on his first flight on the afternoon of August 30. He made it to a height of 2,000 feet, and then he circled the city.

From what I heard and read, George put on a really good show during the fair. He flew his airplane for a long time, then he did sharp dives and vertical pull-ups. The crowd got excited and jumped to its feet.

On September 1, 1911, George took a large number of messages that were addressed to the different officials of the fair. Once he was high up in the air above the fair grounds, he let them go. The crowd ran around and gathered up the messages, then delivered them to the correct officials.

Well, there is the story of the only air delivery of mail before the day I received the card for Mrs. Levenson-Gower from her relatives in Bromley, Kent in the United Kingdom.

All the tricks the biplane was used for in those early days bothered me. I used to read about the latest demonstrations in the different cities in Canada. I thought that they could be doing more with the airplane. Doing tricks for crowds suggested that the airplane was just a toy. When they decided to use the biplane for mail, that was exciting.

Now by airmail, I don't mean that the postcards were picked up in Kent and flown to Canada. Biplanes couldn't fly across the Atlantic yet. The postcard was picked up in London and then flown to Windsor by air. After that, the card was taken by steamship to Canada and by rail to Traynor, Saskatchewan. The card had gone all that way through three different kinds of transportation for two halfpennies!

The postcard had a special picture on it too. It was a picture of a Farman type biplane flying over Windsor Castle. On top were the words, "A.D. — Coronation — 1911 — First U.K. Aerial Post — By sanction of H.M. Postmaster General." The line on the bottom of the picture could be on any piece of mail today. It read, "For conveyance by airplane from London to Windsor. No responsibility in respect of loss, damage, or delay is undertaken by the Postmaster General."

That was the real story of the first airmail to arrive in Canada. There is no doubt about it; I was the one who delivered it here in Traynor, Saskatchewan.

6. Flying Faster Than a Motorcycle?

The way I saw it when I began flying in 1910, the sky was a stage that was free for the taking. I began flying for the sport of it, but the thought of being at the center of the summer fairs was never too far from my mind. My name is Frank Coffyn. I didn't think that there was any other use for biplanes because they were small and didn't have too much power. A biplane really had to work hard to just pull one person into the air. I wasn't sure if anything large could be carried.

I shouldn't imply that I had no fear. I was not one of those free spirits who threw myself into flying in those early days when biplanes were more like kites than machines. When I took my first flight, I was nervous. Even when I took my first flight in Indianapolis, Minnesota with a crowd of 40,000 watching I was still scared. I had a Wright biplane. Even though Wilbur Wright was there helping he actually ran along guiding the wing as I took off I was still uncomfortable.

I realized that the thrill of flying also had the potential to make me a great showman. The crowd was struck with awe when I took to the sky. Few had seen a biplane fly before. With this flight, my name would be remembered in bigger-than-life terms. I was sure that I would become one of the foremost aviators in North America— that was if I could successfully land the biplane— I did.

One of the most exciting places I went to fly was Winnipeg. I guess one of the reasons I went there was that the people had seen less modern machines there. The car was a bit newer there. Even the gas motor was still a mystery to some. When I arrived with the newest of machines, a biplane, people were awe struck. The feeling of excitement and mystery remained through to the end. I would say it even increased as more and more people saw me fly each day I was there.

There were many differences between the field I had to take off in Winnipeg and the fields I used in the United States. In the States, the fields were often as smooth and trimmed as the infield of a baseball diamond. They were flat and well kept. In Winnipeg, the field looked like a thick clover crop that had been mowed only the day before. The greens were as high as my ankles. I liked that because it was soft and smelled like a fresh summer day. The sweet smell of clover and fresh cut grass was in the air everywhere.

There were also fewer telegraph lines around the exhibition grounds. I always hated all the wires I saw around the fair grounds in the States. The only problem in Winnipeg was the high winds.

I arrived in Winnipeg on July 12, 1911 with Ed, my mechanic and Andy, my doctor. I was paid well enough to bring them along. It made me feel better. I was ready for anything.

We were ready to fly on July 15, the first day of the fair. There was one major problem — the wind.

"What do you think, Ed?" I asked as we finished checking the Wright biplane for my first flight.

"Well, I think we should leave this biplane tied down for a while," said Ed as he tightened a bolt on a cross strut.

"That's a good idea."

"The wind is strong enough to catch a wing and flip the machine over. You wouldn't get off the ground if you tried to fly," said Ed as he dropped the wrench he was using.

"The wind might settle down a bit this afternoon," said Andy. "We can promote your flight in the crowd."

"We can get into the fair and enjoy ourselves," said Ed.

* * *

As it turned out, I couldn't fly at all the first day. I spent much of my time by my biplane answering questions and letting farm boys sit in the pilot's seat. They were excited and asked again and again how to become a pilot. Many said that it would be great if they could fly *safely*, even if the distances weren't that great.

The second day was calm. There was a warm breeze with only a few clouds in the sky. I couldn't wait to get into the air. Since we had made the biplane ready to fly the day before, it only took a few moments to get the motor running. I pointed the biplane down the stretch of grass as the crowd quickly gathered. I would have a chance to take two good flights today. The machine made of canvas and string bounced a couple times before I felt the lightness of flight. I was free to ascend into the clouds and thrill the crowd far below.

The Wright biplane lifted me higher and higher until I was in the clouds. I circled around and descended toward the crowd. Everyone looked afraid and unsure for a moment, then I turned to the right and flew upward again. While I was still low, I pushed the biplane into a nosedive. I imagined for a moment that people gasped, thinking I would crash. I pulled up comfortably, waving my wings a little to keep people guessing. Was he okay? I did that once more before I ascended to a higher level, circled once again, and prepared to land. It wasn't too long before I was bouncing along the grass again.

The motor was just slowing down when the crowd moved in close to the biplane. I switched the motor off, and then faced the crowd to answer their questions.

"Did you nearly crash, sir?"

"No, not at all. It was a simple stunt," I said to the wide-eyed boy.

"These machines must be very unstable..." said another man.

"Not that unstable, sir," I replied.

30

"I don't figure I will be flying around in one of these in my day."

"Maybe not," I said.

"These things sure don't seem to go very fast," said a man in a suit.

"What did you expect?"

"Well, it seems to me that if that machine goes up in the air where there is nothing to slow it down, that is nothing except air, you should be able to go faster than a motorcycle."

"Well, of course it goes faster than a motorcycle," I said.

"Hey, you may be able to go faster than a motorcycle, but you can't go faster than a car," said a man in a pair of overalls.

"I am sure that I can fly it faster than a car," I said to the two men.

"You want to try to prove that?" asked the first man.

"I'll tell you something, you can watch my next flight this afternoon. If you think that you can win in a race, you meet me here after the flight. We can decide when and how to race."

"That sounds fair to me," said the man in the overalls.

"I can go along with that," said the other.

With that, the two walked away discussing the proposition. I had raced in a number of races before. They were close. The fair organizers always liked it because a race is always a good show. Everyone can understand a race and enjoy it.

It really never mattered if the pilot lost the race either. It seemed to me that the crowds liked it better if the biplane lost. That meant flying did not have to be taken too seriously. The airplane was only for entertaining at summer fairs. If the biplane won, that was another situation. Did that mean that the biplane would take the place of the car? Would the people across the country have to learn to fly and buy their own aircraft?

It was clear to anyone who was around airplanes that many people were frightened of the thought of flying. My Wright biplane could carry a passenger. Even though I offered everyone the opportunity to fly with me, I had only a handful try it.

When I landed the biplane the second time for the day, I didn't see the two men that challenged me earlier. I was sure that there wouldn't be a race when they came out of the crowd.

"Well, what do you think about a race now?" I asked as they stepped closely to the biplane.

"We'll do it," said the man in the overalls.

"Really? You think that this machine flies that slow?"

"We watched you again. We both think you can't win a race," said the man in the suit.

"Well, if that is what you think, then we have to race," I said as I heard someone begin to chuckle behind me. I turned and look at a man in a suit and a tie.

"You don't think that it is possible that the airplane can win a race?"

"I have no idea, but I do hope that you boys race a McLaughlin."

"Why would you want that make of car in the race?" I asked.

"I'm W.C. Power. I am on the staff of McLaughlin-Buick Motors of Winnipeg."

"I suppose you like the idea of a good advertisement for your cars," I said. "You want to sponsor the race?"

"No, I can't say that's what I want at all. I don't even know these boys here."

"Well, that's right," said the man in the overalls.

"We will need a place to run the race," I said.

"No problem. We can use the race track right here at the fair grounds."

"That is a good idea," I agreed.

"Well then, we will be ready tomorrow."

"That sounds fine to me," I replied. I decided that I was going to fly as hard as I could to win this race. These two men were a little too sure of themselves. I could let them win by flying a little wide on the turns, but on this race I planned to fly tight corners at top speed.

"You believe these boys will win?" I asked as I turned to Mr. Power.

"I'm not a betting man, but I'll tell you something; if you win the race tomorrow, I'll go up with you on a flight."

"That is my prize for winning the race?" I asked.

"Well, I'll bet there will not be a single soul willing to go up with you before this fair is over otherwise."

"Perhaps," I said.

33

"Maybe you could prove to some of these people that flying is safe."

"With that flight, you might get a lot more people interested in flying."

"All right, you're on. If I win the race, you have to be my passenger on the last day. I certainly hope that you don't expect me to lose."

"That sounds good to me," he replied.

"Very well. We will announce when I win the race that you will be flying with me on my last flight of the fair."

"A deal is a deal," he said as he shook my hand.

I liked Mr. Power's attitude.

The time for the race came. There was a large crowd of people at the racetrack as Ed and I pushed the biplane into position.

"Good luck," said the man as he got his motorcycle going. My engine was roaring along with the motors of the motorcycle and the car. I couldn't hear the starter call "ready," but saw his mouth move. Without a pause, the gun fired. Dirt spit out from behind the wheels of the motorcycle and the car. I pushed the throttle forward and let the biplane pull ahead. The two machines rushed out in front of me, gaining a lot of distance.

It didn't take long to get airborne. I felt the resistance of the biplane as I pressed forward as hard as I could. After one lap of the track, I was just overhead of the car. The motorbike was already behind. I wanted to stay low and pull tight on the corners. I got a few feet ahead of the car on the second round. I had to keep myself tense and careful. Again, I pulled hard on the corners. I had to stay in front of the car for four laps. We just finished the third lap. All I could do now was hold a tight course and let the biplane go. I could see the finish line, but I had no idea where the car was. I burst over the finish line and flew higher. I had won the race by twenty yards. Not much, but enough to win. I flew around the track once more and landed. When the biplane's motor was silenced, the clapping quit. People were already leaving the grandstands.

There was Mr. Power waiting for me. He shook my hand as I stepped out of the biplane seat. There was no sign of the car or the motorcycle.

"Well, what do you think now?" I asked. I expected him to back down.

"I will fly with you on the last day."

"That's good to hear," I said.

"Hey, Frank," called Andy as I started looking the biplane over to make sure it was ready for the next flight.

"Is there something wrong?" I asked.

"No," he said. He handed me a piece of paper.

"What is this?" I asked. I opened it and noticed that the T. Eaton Co. logo was on the top.

"A boy delivered it to me during the race. He said that it was another job if we wanted it."

"It is a flying job. They are asking if we want to fly a distance for a prize."

"What is the distance?" asked Ed. He walked around the biplane when he saw the message. "The tank isn't big enough to carry fuel to go too far."

"It says that the distance is about sixty miles to a town called Portage la Prairie."

"How much do they want to pay?" asked Andy.

"They are offering $1,000."

"Well, I don't know. Frank. You know that isn't high enough for the Wright Company," said Ed.

"Yes, I know. I am representing the Wright Company here too. I wander if I should do it. It wouldn't be much of a flight. Even if money isn't that good, it makes a nice addition to the trip."

"You can't do that Frank," said Andy.

"Why not?" I asked.

"Because this is Canada…" stated Ed.

"What does that have to do with it?"

"The Wright Company will know about it in a day."

"Why?"

"That would be a Canadian distance record. In the United States, no one would notice because there are distance records much longer than that," said Ed.

"What we can do is say that the prize is too low. Maybe someone else will offer a higher prize," said Andy.

"I guess that sounds good. Andy, can you make that reply to the Eaton Company and tell the rest to the local newspaper?" I asked.

"Yes, I can do that."

I was sure that there would be no other offers in time to make the distance flight. Even if I wanted to make that flight, I couldn't. There was only one day left. I had a passenger to give a ride to. I was not sure if Mr. Power would be there, but I would be ready for him just in case.

The last day arrived. There had been no new offers for the distance record. I really didn't expect one now. I was up early, getting my biplane ready. In a few hours, I would be finished in Winnipeg and move on. I had two flights to make. In only a few minutes, I would take to the air for the first flight.

I took one last look at the morning crowd at the fair grounds to see if Mr. Power was there. He wasn't. I pushed the throttle forward and headed down the field. In a moment, the biplane lifted from the grass and I was free to fly again.

As the biplane bounced along the grass, I noticed the crowd closing in to look at the machine as usual. Right in front of the crowd was Mr. Power. I decided that I would be ready to go on the second flight in an hour. I wasn't going to let him get away.

"Hello," Mr. Power called as the motor of the biplane became silent.

"Are you ready to fly?"

"I sure am. I would have been here for the morning flight, but I had trouble getting here."

"That's okay. We will have the airplane ready to go in an hour or so."

"That's great," replied Mr. Power with more enthusiasm than I had expected.

Ed went to work to get the biplane ready for the next flight. Mr. Power stayed by the aircraft as we prepared to go up again.

After only forty-five minutes had passed, with the engine started again, I was ready to take Mr. Power up.

"That was real fast work." he said over the loud roar of the engine. I showed him where he was to sit. He settled in quickly. Before he could change his mind, I pushed the throttle forward and the motor roared even more loudly. We skipped down the grass. In a moment, we were lifting off the ground.

I had to concentrate on the take-off because the extra weight. Once we were up, I looked over to where Mr. Power was sitting. I was expecting to see a white and frightened face, but what I saw was a look of excitement. Mr. Power slowly looked from side to side and appeared to enjoy the sights far below. You would never know he was from the prairies. You would expect such a man to love the ground too fondly. Even when I banked the wings hard for turns, Mr. Power appeared to be enjoying himself.

Before long, we were skipping along the ground and coming to a stop.

Mr. Power stood up slowly and smiled. "That was great, sir," he said as he put out his hand to shake it.

"I'm glade you enjoyed yourself."

"Oh, I did. I hope we can do it again."

"We'll be sure to do that if I return next summer."

"That sounds good," he said.

* * *

We did not fly together again. I decided to get my flying license. I received the twenty-sixth certificate issued by the Aero Club of America — the agency that certified pilots in those days. Later, I designed the first pontoons for the Wright biplanes so that biplanes could land on water. I also built an electric movie camera and put it on the bottom of my biplane. I then filmed my flight over the city of New York. That was the first time that had ever been done.

During the Second World War, I worked with the Canadian Aviation Bureau in New York. We hired American pilots to fly aircraft across the Atlantic for the Allied war effort.

Even though a lot of time passed, I always remembered those days in Winnipeg in the summer of 1912.

7. The Biplane that Fell Apart in the Sky

When you start something new, it can go one of two ways. When I started flying as a barnstormer, it did not go well!

I am Dider Masson, an aviator who was just beginning my career in 1911. I was living in Honolulu, Hawaii, when I heard the stories about flying machines. I read every newspaper report I could get. I knew that I wanted to be a pilot, but there was no chance of that in Hawaii. I decided to go to San Francisco where I was sure I could find the help I needed to become a pilot.

In San Francisco, I found two trustworthy mechanics: James Archibald and Jules Brille. We built a Curtiss-type biplane with a rotary, air-cooled, Gnome engine. The whole project cost me $5,000; that was a lot of money in those days, but I got a professionally finished biplane.

Next, I had to figure out how to fly. I talked to the two mechanics. Together we came up with a set of procedures I needed to know to take off and to land. That was all I needed for the moment.

I began slowly by taxiing the biplane down the field and figuring out the controls, then I was flying. The machine responded well. I felt confident that I could fly it.

Well, I had not been flying very long when the *Calgary Herald* invited me to fly at their Aviation Meet. I was the only one flying at this *meet*. They may have planned to have a number of pilots there, but it didn't turn out that way. I arrived in Calgary in October 1911. It was cold, especially for me. Hawaii wasn't at all like Canada in the winter.

Not only was I subjected to the cold Canadian winds; I also had to use the only fuel around — common, low-grade fuel used in cars. The Gnome engine didn't handle the change in fuel very well. It was temperamental at the best of times. To keep the fuel warm, I pulled the fuel line off the outside of the injection chamber, and pushed a pipe through the crankcase. I was able to push the pipe through the hollow crankshaft of the motor. It was risky to do, but it worked. I had no further problems with the fuel after that.

The most important task I had to do was to complete a flight from Calgary to Edmonton. That's not too far, but so little had been tried with biplanes that it would have been a distance record for Canada.

When I arrived, I set up my tent on the open prairies, in a spot right along side of the McLeod Trail.

I made my first flight on October 17. Everyone was excited and satisfied with my demonstration. Actually, all I did was take off and land.

That simple flight was one of the only successful that autumn. On the next day, I prepared to make another flight. When the engine was warmed up, I was ready to go. I pointed the biplane out onto the field that was covered with long grass. I pushed the throttle forward and began taxiing. In no time, I had the biplane moving at top speed. Just as I was about to pull the stick and take off, I heard a muffled sound. The biplane swerved hard to the left, jarring me in my seat. I had hit something. It was a spool of binding twine that someone had left in the long grass! I watched helplessly as the twine was thrown upward and tangled with the propeller and the bamboo struts of the tail wing. The damage to the propeller and the struts had to be repaired. There was no bamboo, but there was wood to do the repairs. We worked on the machine until it was ready to fly.

After that, we walked along the field to check for anything that could get in the way of a good take off before I attempted to fly. Once we were sure that the ground was clear, I boarded the biplane and started the motor. I bounced along the field, and barely made it off the ground. My biplane did not let me down. It rose evenly until I was directly over the center of the city at 2000 feet. I kept going until I reached 14th Street, and then I made a wide circle and flew back to the fair grounds at Victoria Park.

With this flight, I was sure I was ready for the main event—the flight to Edmonton. The flight to Edmonton kept being postponed because the organizers wanted to have a train follow me. To keep a speed of fifty miles an hour, the train had to have only one coach on it. The tracks also had to be cleared of all other traffic right to the city of Edmonton. There were other problems too. The wind was gusting when I tried to take off, pushing the plane into a fence. I was lucky because only one strut was broken. The strut was fixed and then I was on my way again.

When I took off, it was bitter cold as I ascended to a height of 2,000 feet. The cold was too much; I had to land the biplane.

The last chance to attempt the long flight came on October 26. I started the motor and prepared to take off. I felt sure that all the problems had passed. I was not going to let the large crowd at Victoria Park down. The biplane rocked as I rushed down the field and took off. As I flew higher, my confidence grew. This was it! I was going to Edmonton.

Without a warning, the wires that held the fuel tank snapped. The tank came tumbling down on my shoulder. It pushed me forward so that I barely had any room to move the stick in front of me. I tried to move carefully and land the machine.

Just as I was preparing to maneuver the biplane down, the wheels and undercarriage that had been a little broken up in the earlier mishaps broke loose and hit the propeller. In seconds, both tips of the propeller had snapped off. I was still within gliding distance of Victoria Park. I strained under the weight of the fuel tank to turn the biplane around. I forced the nose of the machine around and came into a bumpy landing.

That was my last flight in Canada for a while.

8. Setting a Canadian Record

You probably don't know me. I'm Glenn Martin. Some say that I'm a world-class aviation pioneer.

I remember Saskatoon and those Canadian prairies. I broke the Canadian record for the highest flight there in 1912. That was just at the beginning of my career as an aviator. That was before there were computers and co-pilots to do the flying. We really had to know what we were doing. I designed and built my original pusher biplane in 1909 in Santa Ana, California. I trusted that machine to carry me across America and across Canada.

Of course, we didn't know how fast biplanes could go. We didn't know how long they could fly. My favorite question was the one I settled in Saskatoon, at least for some years; how high could I fly a biplane? Other pilots like Jimmy Ward, who had just flown in Regina a few days before, reached a height of 6,000 feet, but I knew I could do better than that.

Like I said, I started out by designing my own flying machine in 1909. It was a beauty—a biplane with one propeller behind the wings. That's why it was called a pusher.

When I arrived for the annual Exhibition in Saskatoon on August 5, 1912, I knew something was going to happen. It was my day. The city folks crowded around the machine. Some children pushed this way and that to figure out how the rudder worked. I got rid of them as soon as I could. I didn't need problems with the plane before I had a chance to go up. It seemed to me that the further west I went, the more enthusiastic the people were.

From talking to the locals, it was clear that ever since St. Henry's short flights the year before and the news of Jimmy Ward's flight at the Regina fair on August 1, the town people were excited. They wanted to watch me fly. Actually, they didn't care who they saw as long as they saw one of the crazy aviators fly. On the first days of the fair, I let the people look at the biplane and ask questions.

"What does it feel like?"

"Wonderful. Like a bird." They all nodded. "When you are flying you forget what it's like to walk on the ground. You feel weightless. I guess, it's a feeling of being completely free," I try to explain to the group.

"Sir, how do you change directions?"

"With the rudder, like a boat, but more like a speed boat that tips to one side as you turn the rudder."

"It looks hopeless. Just get a horse," says a man in overalls and a straw hat. I just smile at him.

48

"Do you think everyone will have a machine like this some day?"

"No," I replied. The same questions always are asked before I fly. I don't really think that I could answer very many of them because no one really knew how to answer them yet.

On the first day of the fair, I didn't do too much. I wanted to get used to the place and to make sure that the machine was working the way it was supposed to. If I had attempted to break all the Canadian height records on the first day, everyone would want to see a record flight every day after that. That's why I left the Canadian record to the last day. I told no one about my plans either.

On the last day of the fair, I was ready for my attempt to break the Canadian height record. As I unlocked the wheels and pushed the accelerator, the airplane began to move forward. Everyone was expecting to see Glenn Martin fly a circle then a figure eight and then, as usual, land. I pushed the biplane hard after I took off. I wanted to gain as much height as fast as I could. I had only so much fuel and it had to take me all the way up and hopefully most of the way, if not all the way, down to the ground.

My arms ached as I pulled the biplane into a difficult incline. I circled slowly. My ears hurt as I gained altitude. I was going to make it. The motor could overheat at any moment, but I didn't think about that because I was going to beat that Canadian record set by Jimmy Ward. I had to get higher than 6,000 feet. I looked down, I was higher than ever before: 5,900 feet and rising. The needle of the altimeter was going up. I planned to blow the motor if I had to. I could glide the machine down if that happened. I crept higher. It was not be good enough to equal 6,000 feet. I had to go higher! The motor roared at full throttle. I could do it! The machine kept rising. I was over the record by a few feet, then by few more feet. The airplane continued to rise higher and higher. When the motor coughed, that was it. I wasn't sure if the engine was overheated or out of fuel.

It was exciting to be that high. The houses were specks. I could reach out and touch the clouds. I flattened the biplane out and watched for a moment. I took no more chances. I switched the motor off, and then spiraled in wide circles to the ground.

The crowd clapped and whistled more loudly that day than any other. However, few of the satisfied Saskatoon citizens realized that I reached 6,400 feet; 400 feet higher than the previous Canadian record until the Saskatoon *Phoenix* told them on August 10, 1912.

* * *

I came back to Saskatoon in the summer of 1913, the year after I broke the Canadian record for flying the highest. The old pusher biplane I used in 1912 was left behind. This time, I had my newly designed fuselage-type tractor biplane. It looked more like a modern airplane and less like a kite than the aircraft I had a year before. It was fitted with a ninety-horse power Curtiss motor. The most important change was that it could carry a passenger. The locals, who remembered my record-breaking performance, could now fly with me. The funny part was that I could only get one woman and two men to go for a ride.

I always liked it when I first arrived at another summer fair. The grass seems greener and the popcorn fresher. I felt that way when I arrived in Saskatoon. People had that first day excitement.

"Nice to see you fly mister, but there is no way I'm going with you."

"What? Go up there with you?"

"A man has his own feet and maybe a horse to get around on, but he doesn't have wings. What you're doing is most unnatural." Only a few overcame their feelings of suspicion and fear.

I found out that Saskatoon had the beginning of the first registered flying company in Canada. They called it the First Saskatoon Aviation Company.

The man promoting the plan for the company, Hartney, already had a shed built for the company planes. I would never have guessed that Saskatoon would be the first city in commercial aviation in Canada, especially when I could get only three people to fly with me.

I was thinking about that when I was flying at the fair. I looked down and saw all the people staring up at me. They were all dreaming of being up here, but they just couldn't take the first step into the biplane yet. As I looked beyond the fair ground buildings, it struck me. In that wide prairie, getting from one place to the next was tough. They're down there walking or riding a horse and thinking about how good it would be to just fly over the prairie to where they wanted to go. How liberating that would be to have a biplane like this one.

51

You could fly to a farm more than twenty miles away in just a few minutes.

After my first day of flying at the fair, Hartney offered me his shed.

"We don't have any airplanes yet," he said. "You can use the shed for your biplane."

"Are you sure?"

"Of course. I think that you make people want the company here. But I think that we need more excitement to get enough interest to get this place up and running."

"What is you company going to do?"

"It is going to be a flying school."

"Good idea."

"Glad you think so. We are hoping to have an English airman with a Farman biplane come out here to teach lessons."

I was excited by the idea. Flying wouldn't grow too quickly if all the flyers had to build their own biplanes and teach themselves to fly. I expected a lot of companies like Hartney's to start up. There would also have to be companies to manufacture biplanes. Flying was developing fast. I built my first flying machine just four years ago. That machine was just tubing and canvas. Now, most biplanes were built with wood. Yet, certain attitudes were slowing down the development of flying. Three locals going for rides were not enough. Some day, when the novelty wears off, there won't be any demonstrations at summer fairs.

For the rest of the fair, I flew for the crowds and attempted to get more riders. Later, back in the United

States, I flew the same tractor biplane I used in Saskatoon to 9,800 feet. It was a new record.

9. Billy Stark and His Flying Machine

I am Billy Stark and when I started flying in 1912, I was the second Canadian to receive a pilot's license from the Aero Club of America. Of course, in those early days a license wasn't required. Many pilots flew without any kind of license. They would have had to travel to the United States to get their license.

I always liked machines. Some people said I was the first to drive a car with a gas engine in Vancouver. I really don't know if that was true, but when I drove my car down the streets in 1901, I didn't see any other cars.

In 1911, flying seemed like a good sport to me. I decided to look into biplanes. The top man in the business who was teaching others to fly and to build airplanes was Glenn Curtiss in San Diego, California.

Early in 1912, I began flying at the Glen Curtiss School. Flying seemed to come natural to me. I had my pilot's license on March 22, 1912. As soon as I had the license, I bought a new Curtiss exhibition biplane with a seventy-five-horse power motor in it. I took my biplane back with me to Vancouver. I was ready to go to the summer fairs.

The first place I flew in Canada was at the Minoru Park racetrack just south of Vancouver. I was to fly there on April 12, 1912. The warm air smelled of seawater. The track was a perfect surface to take off from. I flew to a height of 500 feet and stayed in the air for twenty minutes. The crowd was excited. The biplane was new to the local people, but few of them took note even though the local newspaper, the *Daily Province*, ran full coverage of the event. The newspaper had a much bigger story on the front cover: the *Titanic*, said to be the greatest ship ever built, had sunk in the north Atlantic.

My first advertised exhibition took place at the same park on April 20. The advertising worked. A huge crowd came out to watch. The British Columbia Railway had to run extra nine cars to carry all the people who wanted to go to Minoru Park.

I took the Curtiss biplane up three times to heights between 400 and 800 feet. The longest flight was thirteen minutes. The one stunt that the crowd liked the most was when I would go up to about 600 feet and then cut the engines and glide, diving to a spot just in front of the grandstand. Just as I got close to the ground, I would pull up hard and make a perfect landing.

The whole time I was training in the United States, I thought it would be great if I could take a passenger along. It was fine to show the people how to fly, but that just was not good enough as far as I was concerned. I wanted to take someone else up with me. The question was where could I put another person? I thought about the question every time I took the biplane up. Then, when I was flying on April 20, it came to me. Why couldn't I just place another person on the wing right beside me? I decided to do that, but finding someone to go along with it would be difficult.

Just as I was thinking about this, I stopped to talk to a sports reporter from the *Daily Province*, James T. Hewitt.

"I really do not know what else I could say to describe flight to you," I said as he pressed me for my impressions.

"Well, I wish I could go along once. I could get to know how it feels for myself." That was it—I had my man. He would be the first to go up with me.

"James, I think I can do that for you. If you think you are up to it, I could make some modifications to the biplane. In a few days, we could take a flight together."

"You mean you would take me up with you? On that same biplane you flew today?"

"All you have to do is hang on and trust me."

"I haven't heard of anyone else ever doing that."

"I think it has been done, but if you don't think you are up to it —"

"No, I didn't say that."

"It's on then."

"Well —"

"We can do it on the 20th."

"All right, I guess so," said James.

"I had to move fast to rig up the seat I had been thinking about. James would probably change his mind if I didn't get him into the air as soon as possible.

I was lucky. I was able to get the seat installed and James sitting beside me on the morning of April 24th.

"You are really going to do this, aren't you?" he asked.

"Of course"

"I had put it out of my mind for the last few days. I really didn't think this was going to happen."

"As you can see, James, the seat is on the wing. You have to sit there and grab onto the strut that is right in front of you. Whatever you do, don't let go!" I shouted over the roar of the motor. He sat down on the wing, looking a little pale. I really didn't have anything to worry about. He wasn't going to let go. He was wearing his black suit and tie and a large white cap with a black band around it.

I watched him for a moment as we began to move down the grassy field. His knuckles turned white as he grasped to the strut. It would be a short flight. The biplane had no problem taking off. I flew up until we reached a height of 600 feet, landing after eight minutes. That was all James could handle.

James wrote a long article about his flying experience that was published in the *Daily Province*. I was surprised that suggested he was more afraid of driving in an automobile than flying in the biplane. "The turning of the machine gave me the feeling of sweeping around a sharp corner in an automobile, but I felt satisfied because I knew there could be no collision around the turn. In fact, I felt much safer than in a Vancouver street."

That was the first time that a flight with a passenger occurred west of Winnipeg. After that, I made some improvements to the seat and talked my wife into being the second passenger. Well, the flight lasted six minutes. My wife became the first woman in Canada to fly as a passenger.

I decided that I had to get closer to my audience, closer to Vancouver so that more people could come to the shows. I decided to go to Hastings Park racetrack. It was not a good place to fly. On three sides, there were large firs and cedars that were difficult to clear. On the fourth side was the open water of Burrard Inlet. Added to this were the huge tree stumps in the infield. I had no place to go if I made the slightest mistake in my landing.

I went ahead with the exhibition at Hastings Park on May 4, 1912. I was right about the location. It brought in a huge number of people.

The first time I took my biplane up, the flight lasted only five minutes. Once I began to feel more comfortable, I prepared to make a longer flight. I took off and climbed to a height of 1,000 feet. I made a few figure eights in the sky, and then dove down to make a careful landing. As I came in closer to the infield where I was planning to land, I couldn't believe what I saw. I front of me was a whole herd of cattle. The crowd was watching me up in the sky and not looking at the field in front of them. A few of the animals went crazy and ran right into the path of the biplane. I looked in front and realized the high trees made it impossible to ascend and that I couldn't get high enough to clear them. Ahead, I could see only a wood fence and my two helpers on the ground. I put the wheels of the biplane down on the ground and jumped out of the biplane only twenty feet before it crashed into the fence.

My two helpers tried to grab the wings of the biplane to avoid the inevitable crash. Perry, the first of my two assistants, had a badly cut hand. Watson was knocked down and run over by the biplane, but he only had a few bruises after the incident. I don't think I had anything more than bruises either.

The next show I had was for an exhibition at Victoria on May 24th. I assembled my biplane and then glided along the wet grass to a perfect take off. I flew for twenty minutes. To land, I dipped and dove toward the ground until I was touching it. I pushed the wheel brake, but it made no difference. On the wet grass, I slipped along as though I didn't have a brake at all. In front of me was another fence! Just like before, I jumped from the biplane. In a moment, I heard the muffled crashed of the biplane. This time, the Curtiss biplane was severely damaged.

The crowd didn't mind that I could not make the second flight that day. The local newspaper even published a good review of the flight. We had the biplane repaired by the next day for an afternoon flight. This time, I flew for fifteen minutes, and then made a good landing.

My next exhibition was to be held at Armstrong, BC on July 1, 1912. We put the biplane together in the hockey rink while the locals sat in the bleachers and watched.

When I was ready to go, it was cold and blowing. I didn't feel comfortable taking off in bad weather like that, but I felt I had to. The people had their hopes up. I couldn't let them down. I took the biplane into the air to a height of 1,500 feet and headed down the Otter Lake Valley. I couldn't stop the biplane from rocking and rolling back and forth as I went. After only two miles, I decided to turn back. With the wind pushing me, I flew quickly back to the grounds. I dropped down low as I went through the fair grounds. There wasn't enough room to land there. I had to look for a place beyond the town. I flew on until I found an open field. The biplane came down softly to a safe landing. A motorist stopped and offered me a ride back to the fair grounds.

After that fair, I was asked to go to Portland, Oregon to fly another pilot's machine.

I arrived on a hot summer day to an enthusiastic crowd. I looked at the fair grounds. This place was different than any other I had flown in before. I would be flying over streets and buildings, not trees and open water.

I sat down in the biplane. Soon, the motor was running full throttle. I let the brakes go, took off and lifted off the field. In moments, I could see the grandstands pass behind me. I could see the parking lot when the motor coughed and died. There was a crowd of people just beyond the parking lot, right where I wanted to land. I couldn't land there! All I could do was dive for the cars. I did. Before I could think, I heard the crashing sound around me and it was over. I moved one leg, then the next, and sat up on the pavement. I felt terrible. I looked at my legs. Nothing was broken except the biplane, which was in pieces all around me.

The newspapers praised the landing as a heroic effort to save lives, but I simply could not get into the seat of another biplane. At least, I avoided flying for a couple of years.

10. Canada's First Aerial Distance Record

I'm William Robinson. When I was asked to come to Canada in 1913 to set a distance record for flying, it did not seem out of place at all. The airplane had become quickly accepted around the world. Across Europe and the United States, people as well as governments wanted to know more about the airplane. How far could they go? How high could they go? How fast could the biplane fly? How long could they stay in the air? These were all questions that everyone wanted answers too. Every pilot was attempting new records. Groups often invited airmen to set new records for good pay.

When I arrived in Montreal from the United States in the fall of 1913, the world record for distance was almost six hundred and fifty miles. The record in the United States was 217.5 miles. Canada didn't have a record for distance yet. I thought it was strange that the officials in Montreal hadn't asked one of the Canadian pilots like John McCurdy or Billy Stark from the West Coast. However, I didn't ask too many questions, I just got to my job.

My aircraft was a tractor type biplane that I had designed and built myself. I brought it to Canada in two large packing crates.

I was not asked to attempt a new world distance record. The distance I was asked to fly didn't even get close to the record set in the United States. I was to fly the one hundred and sixteen miles from Montreal to Ottawa. The entire flight was to take a couple of hours.

At ten minutes to ten in the morning on October 8, I was ready to go. The Mayer of Montreal, Mr. Lavalle, handed me a small bundle of local newspapers, the *Daily Mail*. I was to deliver some of these papers to communities on the way to Ottawa. In the last bundle of newspapers were newspapers addressed to the Prime Minister Robert Borden, Sir Wilfred Laurier, Sir Charles Fitzpatrick, and to the mayor of Ottawa, Mr. Ellis.

The air felt cold and misty as I let the motor roar. In moments, I was in the air. I watched a large group of people below pass into the distance as I flew on my course. I was in the air for ten minutes when the motor coughed and began to die. I looked down. I had to land. I brought the biplane down to a smooth landing at Lachine. I stepped down from the biplane and looked at it. I could smell fuel—the fuel line had broken.

"*Bonjour!*" came a call from behind me. I turned and looked at the small man in front of the group. He was wearing a pair of overalls.

"Hello!" I replied.

"We saw you flying overhead. We are all very interested in these machines."

"Oh. Well here is one for you to look at."

"Why did you stop here?"

"The fuel line is broken."

"Is it like an auto?"

"Yes, just like a car. I need a piece of tubing."

"Let me look —" said the short man as he stepped up to the biplane and looked at the tank and the line. He put his hand on the fuel line and pulled on it. The tube broke right away from the tank."

"What are you…"

"Yes, I have a garage," he replied. With that he turned and was gone. I would have to stay by the biplane because the crowd was getting larger by the moment.

"Hey, are you coming right back?" I called after the short man. He kept moving away from us. He had not heard me.

"Hey is he a mechanic?" The group took little notice of me. They continued to walk around the biplane, speaking in French. They pulled at the rigging here and there.

I sat in the pilot's seat. What was I going to do? I leaned back and thought for a moment. I would just sit here for a while and wait. If the short man were not back soon, I would have to walk into the town to see if I can find some tubing for myself.

I stood up. Too much time had passed, I decided. Now I had to walk to town and do something about the fuel line. I stepped away from the biplane in the direction that the small man had walked and looked up and there he was.

"I find the tube," announced the man as he stepped by me.

He went to work without asking any questions. I was surprised at the speed with which he had pulled the old tube off the tank and had the new one installed.

"We have fuel," he announced. A boy stepped to the man's side. He must have been standing there the whole time, but I had not seen him. He had a pail of fuel and a funnel. In moments, the tank was full again.

"You show us now how the machine goes," said the mechanic.

"Yes, I guess I will. Thank you."

"*Oui*," smiled the man. In moments, the motor was roaring again. I pushed the throttle forward, and then went skipping along the field. I flew higher and higher, circling.

I looked down and the group was a speck in the grass. I looked at my watch. It was five minutes after one o'clock.

I was behind time. I still had three scheduled stops. Each had an airfield marked by large white crosses. The first stop was at Choisy. It was already 1:30 in the afternoon by the time I arrived. The crowd and the questions kept me on the ground longer than I had expected. Finally I was skipping along the grass to take off at 2:30 in the afternoon.

The second stop was at the community of Caledonia. I arrived at 2:45. Again my arrival was more like a summer fair than a quick drop of newspapers and an opportunity to refuel. It was five minutes after four when I took off.

The situation did not improve at all. The sky became more and more hazy as I went. The only way I could guide myself was with a rough map the Canadian Pacific Railroad had provided. The map showed the main line, but it was confusing because of the large number of branch lines that had been constructed in the area.

I kept going. Soon, I found that luck was on my side; I saw the grass of Lansdowne Park, the place I was to land. I flew in close to the park and looked down. I wasn't surprised to see that my arrival had attracted a large crowd. I flew in a circle for a while, asking myself if the people were going to move off the field. I hoped they would realize that they were supposed to. I had to fly onto Slattery's field, where there were no people. I landed at five o'clock, a full five hours behind schedule. The group soon swarmed around the biplane, but I was able to deliver the newspapers to Mayor Ellis.

The record was set for distance. Yet, for the people along the line I had flown; the biplane was not the machine with practical uses. It was still a novelty for summer fairs.

11. A Short Lived Passenger Service

I am Jimmy Ward's mechanic, Clair Horton. I had just arrived with Jimmy to put on a demonstration of flying in the spring of 1914 at Winnipeg. We hadn't been in town for long when I ran into Bill Robertson. I had known Bill since 1912 when Jimmie and I had flown at the fair. He walked up to me when I was checking the engine on Jimmy's plane one more time.

The spring air felt hot and muggy. The grass smelled stale as it wilted in the heat. If this is spring, what is the summer going to be like? I wished it were cool and quiet. The crowd was quickly growing at the Winnipeg fair grounds. I wished that I were the one flying that afternoon. I was tired of fairs. I was tired of just being the mechanic.

"Clair, how's it going?" asked Bill.

"Pretty good now that we are here. We had a long boring trip up on the truck. The roads were just dusty cow paths."

"I can understand that. It has been a dry, hot spring. I'll bet the whole summer will be like that."

"We are planning to fly in all the shows on the prairies and the mid-western states. I hope the weather cools down a little."

"You sound like you are a little tired."

"The summer fairs are something. We have been touring for three years or is it four? It doesn't matter. We could be flying for a few more years yet. The people still swarm around the biplane," I said.

"You don't seem too excited about flying anymore"

"I am."

"Really? You don't look too happy," said Bill.

"I didn't say I was happy about being on the road all the time, but I like flying. I just got my flying certificate."

"That's great."

"What is getting to me is that the summer fairs are always the same."

"Do you really think that these public demonstrations are going to keep bringing people in?"

"I have been ignoring the crowds in the fairs for the last while. I get the biplane ready for Jimmie to take off, and then I turn around and find something else to do until I'm needed again. I watched some good games and took in some horse shows. Maybe the crowds for the flying shows are getting smaller."

"I think they are."

"Oh? Jimmie still gets the invitations to the flying meets and summer fairs. The money is still good for the work we're doing."

70

"Flying is more common now. People are not as amused and amazed as they used to be," said Bill.

"Bill, what else do you think those planes could be used for?"

"I figure that we could start using them like cars."

"Everyone with a flying certificate? I can't believe that."

"No, not each person using his own airplane, but maybe private flying companies offering rides to those who need to go some place fast."

"Or maybe, flying people over water or bush."

"Yeah, that is what we could do," said Bill.

"*We* could do what?"

"We could set up a flying company together. That is a good idea we came up with."

"Bill, how long have you been trying to get someone to help you with this project?" I asked. Bill smiled.

"Well, for awhile, but it would take a man of foresight to set up a company like that."

"Yeah, just like the summer fair demonstrations. I believed they would never end."

"Transport with biplane has many possibilities. Everything that is moved by cars, horses, and even trains could be moved by airplane some day."

"We should just talk about people for now."

"I'll count you in then."

"Okay. By the way, how many other people have you talked into helping you form this company?"

"Just you."

"Good to know, I guess," I said. Bill turned and walked away.

* * *

I watched as Jimmie directed his biplane down the grass of the Exhibition Grounds. I turned and began walking toward the concessions before he lifted from the ground.

"Getting away from the flying, Clair?"

"Hello Bill," I said.

"We need to make some plans about that company we're forming."

"I just agreed to help you with it this morning."

"It seems like a long time. I think we better get it settled soon because most of our business will be in the summer."

"Yeah, I figure it would be. There isn't much hope of having a winter service here in Canada."

We walked across the field to a nearby café. We sat down and waited for the waitress. The sound of the distant hum of Jimmie's biplane was in the background.

"Do you gents want anything here?"

"Two Denver sandwiches and coffee," said Bill. It is on me," he said as the waitress turned and walked away.

"Thank you."

"Clair we need some biplanes," said Bill.

"What did you figure this company is going to do?"

"Offer people flying transportation."

"I guess we need a tractor-type Curtiss with two seats."

"That is a good half of what I figure we can use."

"Do you have something else in mind?"

"I figure most of our customers will want to fly from Victoria Beach on Lake Winnipeg. The kind of people who want to get to the resort fast and have the money to pay to get there."

"So we need one of those water plans. What do they call them?"

"They are called hydroplanes," said Bill. "We can operate one biplane out of there and a second one out of the Exhibition Grounds."

"I figure we need another pilot."

"I know a guy who just came in from England. He has his flying certificate. We can hire him to fly the land plane."

"What is his name?"

"Mr. Minchin."

"I guess I will be flying the water airplane."

"Yes, that will work."

* * *

It wasn't long before the two biplanes arrived from the Curtiss Company in New York State. They needed a little work, but they were in the air by the last week of June.

I was feeling pretty good on the morning of July 13 as I was getting ready to take my first passengers into the air. I hadn't done much flying before I made Dr. Atkinson of Selkirk comfortable in the passenger seat of the hydroplane. I opened the throttle wide and the motor roared. Everything was operating perfectly. I had been looking forward to this day. In a moment, we were skipping along the lake. I pulled the control stick back and the biplane lifted from the water nicely. The lake looked beautiful as we climbed higher. It was time to level out the flight. I pushed hard on the stick to stop the upward climb.

The stick would not move. I had no idea what was stopping the stick from moving forward. I looked from one side to the next. I noticed that the snap hook we used to hold the controls in neutral while we were parked on the beach was hooked on the turnbuckle of the control wire. To get that snap loose, I had to pull back quickly on the stick and slip the snap free. I wasn't sure if I had enough power in the motor to do it, but there was no choice. I had to get that snap free if I was going to be able to fly the biplane anywhere. I pulled the stick back, but we were already climbing to steep. The biplane stalled. I couldn't help it. The biplane crashed in moments.

I could barely breathe when I reached the surface of the water. The water was much colder than I had expected. It took my breath away. The biplane floated in pieces all around.

The doctor had lost his breath too, but something else was wrong. He had panicked. Red blood stained the water. I grabbed him and dragged him the five hundred feet to the shore. He had a cut on his right arm.

The hydroplane needed a lot of work. The biplane that was flying out of the Exhibition Grounds was also no longer attracting many riders. We decided we had to move on. Once the hydroplane was fixed, we took the entire company and moved to Detroit for the rest of the season. Soon, there was no more work. When the First World War began, we were expected to do other work.

12. The Toronto Aviation School

When the First World War broke out in 1914, I wanted to get into the middle of it. My heart was set on being a fighter pilot. I was about to try flying that summer, but the war came without warning. There were two air services that a potential pilot could join. The first service was the Royal Flying Corps and the next service was the Royal Naval Air Service. Both were based in Great Britain.

My name is Adam McKenzie. I applied through the local militia office at least half a dozen times until it was clear that the only way to get into one of the flying services was to enlist in the army or navy and hope for a transfer. I didn't like that idea at all. I didn't think there was much hope of being transferred after you were in the army and in the trenches.

Another way to get into the Flying Corps was to go to either Farnborough or Rouen in France on your own. Once you were there, you could join up and hope for the best. But, I figured that after I had gone all the way to France, my chances of getting into the flying corps was about the same as in Canada.

Finally, I thought of another way to get into the Royal Flying Corp. That was to go to a flying school and get a flying certificate first, then join the army and ask to be transferred to the Flying Corp.

It was the summer of 1915 when I traveled to Toronto to join the new Curtiss Aviation School that had been established at Long Branch. The school was a part of the Curtiss Company in Hammondsport, New York. The operation was really impressive because it was more than just a school for pilots. The Curtiss Company had also built a factory to produce biplanes in Canada called Curtiss Aerospace and Motors Limited. It manufactured JN Curtiss training planes, the ones that had two seats. Added to that, the school itself had three huge hangers. The sight of biplanes flying around, with some taking off and some landing often attracted large crowds. I stood there with the rest of them, watching. I couldn't believe that the school was that large. I thought for a minute. Could I really get into the school?

There was no way of really knowing until I tried. I stepped out of the crowd and made my way to the huge hangars.

"Hey you!" called a medium sized man with a moustache. My heart pounded as I felt like a kid caught stealing something.

"Yeah?"

"Are you here to sign up to learn to fly?"

"Yes," I said as I felt the nervousness subside.

"Well, have you ever flown before?"

"No," I replied.

"Well, I'll take you up before you register. If you like it, you can register right away."

"Yes, I guess," I said. I had a strange feeling of watching myself and not really being the one who was getting ready to fly. Could this really be happening that fast? I walked up to the side of the hangar and threw down my small suitcase. The motor of the biplane behind me popped. I looked and saw the man who had offered the ride getting his motor started. Another man stood in front of the biplane, grabbed the propeller and pulled it around another time. This time the motor came to life and roared. The man motioned to me.

I rushed to the biplane and pulled myself into the back seat. I had just sat down when I felt the force of the biplane accelerating down the airfield pushing me back. I quickly latched the buckle of the harness.

I couldn't believe the feeling of flying. It was magnificent. The biplane rose to an unbelievable height. We kept rising. As we rose, the air became cold. When I stopped looking down, what I saw made me realize that I wanted to learn to fly no matter what. Right there beside me was the white haze of a cloud. I was no longer lying on the haystack at home on the farm thinking how great it would be to be up there.

After we landed, I stepped down from the biplane. I would have sworn that my feet had not touched the ground.

"What do you think, son?"

"Where do I register?"

"In that far hangar. The office is in the back."

"I don't have any money to pay for lessons, but I'll help around the hangars. I am handy with tools and mechanical things."

"You don't have to worry about that. Just sign a paper saying you will sign up with the Flying Corps in Britain, then you'll be fine."

"Free? I'll register right away."

It only took a short time before I had filled out the papers and signed them. I was going to start flying the next day.

* * *

Early in the morning, the biplanes were already taking off from the airfield. Because I was used to getting up earlier, I was on the airfield before they even had breakfast ready. I held the leather-flying helmet I had been issued. The flying suit wasn't anything more than a pair of overalls. They were like the overalls I had worn on the farm, but they had zippers, not just buttons. I felt real sharp in that clean suit watching the planes.

"Hey kid!" called the man near the hanger. I walked closer and realized the man calling to me was the same one that had taken me up for the ride the day before.

"Yeah?"

"You're here early. What's your name?"

"Adam McKenzie."

"I'm Victor. I'm one of the instructors."

"How do you do?"

"I don't know whom your instructor is going to be, but you can jump in with me for a quick flight before breakfast," he said as we walked to one of the planes.

"Thank you."

"Jump in. You may as well begin your lessons. Don't just ride back there. Keep your hands on the control and get a feel for the way the machine works."

"Sure," I said. In moments, we were skipping down the field, then we were in the air.

It was refreshing to fly. The biplane responded to every movement of the stick. I was surprised at how slow all the movements were. I could move the controls slowly if anything happened.

Like the first flight, it was over too soon. Victor grinned as he lifted himself out of the cockpit.

"Next time, you will be in the front seat."

"Why?"

"You know all that I did was take off and land this machine."

"Oh?"

"You'll do fine," he said.

* * *

"Hey, Adam," called Victor. I was on the tarmac of the runway after breakfast.

"Yeah?"

"It looks like we got a jump on you lessons. We have had our first lesson this morning, now we can continue where we left off."

"Does that mean that you are my instructor?"

"Isn't that something?"

81

"That's good."

"What you need to know is how to take off and land. The rest is just a matter of getting up there and practicing."

"Taking off and landing shouldn't be that bad."

"Those are the worst times for crashes."

"Really?"

"You were supposed to have had your hand on the control to figure out what happens. Do you remember what I did to take off?"

"Sure. You pointed the machine down the field and opened up the throttle and let it go. When you got some good speed, you pulled back on the stick and up it went."

"No, that wouldn't work."

"Why?"

"The back end would be right down on the ground. You would never get your speed up high enough."

"Doesn't the back end just come up?"

"No. You have to push the stick forward as you taxi down the field. Then when the tail is up, you flatten out the wings and speed up. Then, you slowly pull the stick back. We're going up once with you in the front seat feeling the stick. The next time up after that, you can do it yourself."

My chance came in twelve minutes. I concentrated on what I had just learned. I opened the throttle up until the motor roared. I pointed the biplane straight down the field and our speed increased. Then I had to push the stick forward. I pushed it forward slowly until the tail lifted. It worked. The biplane gained speed, but the end of the airfield was coming fast. I had to start pulling up. I had just started to pull back when I felt the lightness of flight. The wheels were off the ground. I felt great, as I pulled further back on the stick. We began to climb. I kept climbing until I could see the clouds so close that I could touch them, and then I flattened out the biplane. I turned the plane right, then I turned left and made a wide circle. I was going to fly as much as I could while I had the chance. I pushed the stick forward and turned to the left at the same time. The biplane dipped and turned to the left. Then, I turned right and pulled up. Feeling the dips and turns was incredible.

I jumped a little when I felt a pat on my shoulder. I turned and looked back. There was Victor with a wide smile. He was giving me a thumb down sign. I complied; I pushed forward on the stick. The airfield was to the left. I kept descending, pushed the stick to the left and turned. I came down in the right place; I kept control of the craft, and gently brought it to the surface of the field. Then, we made contact with the ground. It never felt so hard. We bounced once into the air, but I held firm and let the wheels down. We slowed. I pulled gently back on the stick to bring the tail down. We skidded to a stop.

Victor jumped out of the back seat. I had unbuckled my harness before I heard Victor yelling.

"Adam, take her up on your own! Be sure not to climb too fast!"

I sat back in the seat. Was he telling me that I had to take off again? Or was he asking me if I wanted to?

I turned toward the place he had been standing. He was gone. I was going to ask if I had enough fuel. The motor was still idling. He must have meant it was time to take her up by myself.

I taxied the machine to the end of the field. I couldn't see anyone coming into land. There was no one taking off either. Away I went. The machine bobbed along the ground. In a moment, I was rising up into the air. I looked up high and saw the light puffs of cloud that I had been flying above only a few minutes before. I was going to go around them, but I really wanted to go through one. I pointed the biplane toward the cloud. I rose higher and higher. Just as I thought I was going to hit the cloud, I was in a thick haze. The biplane climbed as I looked around. It felt like I was separated from the plane. I felt like I had my own wings. The fog was gone as fast as it had arrived.

I watched the clouds pass under the biplane. Suddenly, I felt afraid. Remembering that I had lost all sense of time when I flew before, I wondered if there enough fuel to get back. I made a wide circle and headed back. I pushed the stick forward and dropped in height until I had passed through the clouds. I could see now. Now another question bothered me. How would I get back? I hadn't been shown how to navigate. I flew on hoping to find my way back. I began to recognize the roofs of the hangars. I watched intensely for a moment. I realized that I would have to climb a little and circle to the right to line up the plane with the runway.

I felt relieved to see the runway. In moment, I was heading for a landing. I concentrated on the landing. The bounce was small as I came down. I taxied the machine to the same place it had been when Victor left. Victor was there shaking his head and staring at me.

"I'm back!" I called as I pulled myself from the cockpit. I noticed that my flying suit was wet with sweat. I never realized that I was shaking until I lowered myself to the ground.

"This is the first time I have seen that," he said.

"What is that?"

"I always suggest that my students take her up alone on their first day. You are the only one who did it."

"Oh, really?"

"You should have had some trouble."

I didn't have any trouble. It only took two and half weeks before I was told I was ready for my flying test.

"Victor, what are you talking about? What do I have to do on this test anyway?"

"Take the plane up, make a figure eight and then land."

I had heard that the test was that simple, but I never believed it until that day. I guess the real training began when I went to France, but that is another story.

13. Stark Returns to Instruct Pilots for the Great War

As you may know, I'm Billy Stark, a pilot who began flying in 1912. I had a lot of experience in flying at summer fairs and exhibitions after I received my license in 1912. I quit flying after my crashes during the summer of 1912. I began again in 1915 because I felt the time had come for us Canadians to start training more pilots for the First World War. When I started asking for a school, the government had little interest in establishing flying schools in Canada. That was fair enough because the country had to worry more about getting men overseas to the front and about assisting with the war effort as much as possible. Another reason why the government wasn't supporting flying that much was there wasn't yet much evidence to support the argument that the biplane could be an important weapon in war.

87

The truth of the matter was that we, my friends and I, had to build the school and train the pilots for the war by ourselves. In good times, the government and the military would have realized how important the airplane was to war. But with the hurry to get the country's war effort off the ground, there were other things for the officials to consider first.

I decided to build a business to train students who were prepared to pay. Not only did we need a business to train the new pilots, but we also needed an airplane club to issue certificates. All these issues were discussed at a meeting with some of my friends. We decided to form a school and to request that the *Federation Aeronautique Internationale* in France register the school.

We applied to the federation in France immediately. We were also given fast recognition as the Aero Club of British Columbia. Then we had to start building the school. To start with, the school received enough money from a number of people to buy my biplane for $2,500. In addition, the school paid me a fee of twenty-five dollars a week to instruct. Even though we had enough money from public support establish the school, we did not have enough to keep operating. We had to charge the students two hundred dollars for the training.

Even with such a large fee, there were more than enough applicants. We had to train the pilots, but the government assured us that once the pilots were trained, it would pay for the transportation of the men to France.

With the school established, our attention turned to the training. There was one major problem I hadn't quite solved yet. How could I instruct students to fly in a machine that had only one seat? I had rigged a seat on an earlier biplane of mine for my wife to ride on, but that wasn't enough. I would have no control over the plane when a student was flying. With the roar of the motor, I could not issue instructions.

I considered rigging a seat in the back, but realized the biplane would not be balanced.

I began by demonstrating how to fly. I had the students sit in the chair of the biplane and watch what they were doing on the flaps and the rudder. I figured that I could let the students taxi the biplane without taking the risk of them taking off without knowing how to land.

I had been standing by the biplane waiting for Vick, one of my students, to arrive. We were going to have a lesson. I moved quickly to get ready when I saw Vick step out of the shed and walk toward me.

"Hi Bill," he said.

"I'm ready for you," I said.

"Are we going to carry on with movements of the controls again today?"

"In a way. We are going to try something new today."

"What?"

"Get into the seat and strap yourself in."

"Sure," he said as he sat down in the seat.

I stood beside the plane by the pusher propeller that was behind the main wing.

"We are going to begin by starting the motor. I will turn the prop while you choke the motor. After it is going, I want you to pull the throttle backward until the motor turns over as slow as it can go."

"Then what?"

"I'll get up there and tell you," I said.

"Okay, that sounds good."

"Ready?"

"Yes," he said. I pulled hard on the prop. The motor turned over once and died. I put my hand on the prop one more time and pulled hard. The motor sputtered once, then it raced quickly. As I had told Vick, the motor slowed to an idling speed. I walked around the slowly moving biplane and stepped on the wing.

Standing beside Vick I yelled, "Turn the machine around and face the open field!"

Vick complied quickly. In a moment, we were facing the field and moving down it slowly.

"Okay, now, put your hand on the throttle and get that motor going."

"Are you sure?"

"Push that throttle now!" I yelled. I could imagine what Vick was thinking.

The biplane sped up and skipped along the field. Vick was pale and nervous.

"Okay! Slow down!" I called.

Vick did as he was told. We were at the end of the field. I watched for a moment. Did he have enough sense to turn around before we hit the fence? We got turned around.

90

"Okay that looked good. This time I want you to do the same thing in the opposite direction." Vick complied. Soon, we were at a good speed.

"Push the throttle all the way down!" I yelled over the roar of the engine. He did as he was told. The biplane sped up only a little. He pressed the throttle forward harder. He looked at me, unsure. He knew the biplane should go faster to take off. I smiled. He looked forward, then slowed the machine down and turned again because of the shed in our path.

"All right, turn the motor off!" I said. In a moment, the motor made its last groan.

"Why didn't the machine go faster?"

I stepped off the wing and went around to the front of the biplane.

"Vick do you have a pencil?"

"A pencil?"

"Yeah, a pencil," I said. Vick looked bewildered. He reached up to his pocket and pulled out a pencil. He handed it to me. I leaned over in front of him and pulled a wedge of wood out of the throttle mechanism. I held it in up and marked a line on it. I turned it over and wrote *Vick* on the top. I handed the wedge to him.

"You passed that lesson. This is your gas ration wedge. Don't loose it. Before you come to your lesson tomorrow, cut it down that line while you review and steps of taking off. I want you to know about getting the back rudder up off the ground."

"Okay," said Vick.

"On second thought, I think I'll have that wedge back. I will probably cut a straighter line," I said. Vick turned and walked away shaking his head. I had to hurry. I needed to find another wedge for the next lesson.

* * *

Because we needed much more space than we had for the long taxiing we were doing, the school had to be moved from where it was at Lulu Island, just outside of Vancouver. The new field was smooth and even. We named the new runway *Terra Nova*, which was the name of a nearby canning factory. After that, we built a small hangar.

We had everything ready for the lessons in September. Lessons ended in November because it was just too cold. Just before lessons had to be stopped, Lieutenant-Colonel C. J. Burke of the Royal Flying Corps arrived from England to examine my two pilots, Murton and Phil. He arrived in his uniform, looking smart.

"Hello, I'm Bill Stark," I said.

"Yes, I have heard much about you and your school."

"This is Phil and this is Murton," I introduced the two.

"How do you do," he said. "And where is the plane?"

"Right over there," I said as I turned and pointed at the Curtiss pusher biplane we were using.

"Excuse me, where is it?" he asked again.

"Right there."

"You are flying that? That is an old American biplane. It has no closed fuselage on it."

"That's right. We have a small operation. Funds have been restricted," I said.

"If your boys can fly the formations with that machine, they will be indeed good men for the Corps."

"You heard it boys," I said. "Who is going to be examined first?"

"There are only two. Either one can fly first."

"Murton, take the biplane up," I said.

"Sure," said Murton. In moment, the motor was at full speed and Murton was taking off. He flew up and made a perfect figure eight. Murton landed the biplane, and then Phil took off.

"Very good," said Burke. "Both of you are now pilots and I trust that both of you will return with me to England."

"Absolutely," said Phil.

"And I recommend that you obtain a number of better machines as soon as possible," said Burke.

"I couldn't agree with you more," I said.

* * *

With this early success, I was certain that the school was going to expand. The most pressing question I had to answer was how could I continue training pilots through the winter? More pilots were needed. Small schools like mine needed to do much more.

I figured the only way I could continue flying was to move to the warmest part of British Columbia–out on the water. I went over to the motorboat works at Burrand Inlet. I knew the guys who ran the place, the

Hoffer brothers. They agreed to help me convert the biplane into a hydroplane and the changes were soon made. I was ready to start the taxiing lessons with a new pilot. The newly converted biplane worked well. The first lesson took place in no time. I had hardly begun the lessons when I found out the biplane was too small. As in every lesson before, I was on the wing when a student was operating the controls. We were speeding in the water, and then suddenly we were swimming in the water. I looked around as I treaded water. All I could see was a little of the wing that Bob, the new student, was hanging on to. To one side, was the floating log that had tipped us. It wasn't long before the ferry; the *Sonrisa* was on the scene. They pulled us out of the water, wet and cold.

After we pulled the biplane from the water, it was obvious that there could not be any more training until spring. I needed much more than an old pusher biplane and a small hangar to train pilots. The students weren't doing any better than the school. They needed some form of support while they waited. We arranged for them to join the 58th battalion in Vancouver during the winter. They learned wireless and nautical astronomy there.

With the daily routine of instructing put aside, my attention turned to strengthening the school. By December, the Aero Club of British Columbia was reorganized into the British Columbia Aviation School Limited. We offered an issue of non-profit stocks for people to buy to support our school and the war effort. I was certain that the people would respond well and we would be able to buy four two-seater biplanes from the Curtiss Company in the United States at the cost of $15,000.

I was wrong. People in Vancouver did not support the effort very well. We couldn't buy any new Curtiss biplanes, but we did have enough money to buy a two-seater biplane built in Vancouver. It was not much, but at least we could continue with the same number of students as we had the summer before. We would have to wait until the government realized the value of biplanes in war. I believed that we would get the money to expand by the fall of 1916.

I talked with local businessmen to gain more support for the expansion during the winter of 1915. As time passed, it became clear that the people would not volunteer the money. The businessmen began pulling further away from their earlier support of the air school. I thought if they had shown a little more leadership, the situation might have been different. I remember discussing things with Edward, an owner of several stores in Vancouver, about our need for support to make the schoolwork in December 1915.

"Ed you know that things have to start going our way soon. They are going to have to develop better training facilities in Canada for the war."

"I don't know that, Bill. I'm not so sure that the war is going to be won in the air."

"It isn't going to be won by air power. I never said that. Just that air power is going to be an important factor in winning the war. I am sure that Canada is going to have to train a lot more pilots before it is over."

"There just isn't the support among the people to run the school here."

"Aren't you a businessman that has shown initiative in new ventures?"

"I have initiative, but that doesn't mean I'm stupid."

"You are going to let the school die."

"No, not at all. We will have enough money for one biplane. It will be the same as it has been up to this point."

"That isn't good enough."

"It has been fine until now. Why do we need to expand? No one is going to question your patriotism Bill. You are doing all you can."

"With more planes and more instructors, we could do much more."

"We are doing enough. I don't support any further expansion."

"I guess that means we won't do anything else. One biplane is not good enough. With one mishap, the whole school has to shut down."

"I have given you my final word on it Bill. You knew what we could afford."

"To stay here under these conditions is a waste of my time. I said I would resign if this was all we are going to do."

"There is nothing I can do about it."

"You will have to find another instructor then."

"Fine."

* * *

They did find another instructor in the United States, but the school didn't last long. One of the students was sent up on his solo flight, lost control of the aircraft and crashed.

I was right about something else too. The government did eventually invite the Royal Flying Corps to come to Canada and establish what turned out to be one of the biggest air training centers of the First World War.

14. Men With Dash

By 1917, the Royal Flying Corps had arrived in Canada to train pilots for the First World War. I wanted to be a pilot in the war, but because I couldn't see any way of getting into flying, I worked in munitions in Toronto. When I heard that the Royal Flying Corps had arrived, I couldn't wait to get signed up. Before I knew it, I became a pilot and went to England. Following some more "operational" training, I was out over the trenches in 1918.

Our camp was miles behind the front. The guns in the distance sounded like a thunderstorm that never ended. The sound of the explosion was different than the sound of the thunder. Artillery has a more heavy sound without the same kind of echo after it that thunder has. Thunder has more of a rolling sound.

We were glad that we were at a distance, but the thought of how fast we could be on top of the hottest action haunted us. I stared at two other airmen. We

99

were sitting around a fire at our camp drinking our ration of coffee, thinking about the next day's mission.

"Hey Tom, where were you trained to come to this God-forsaken place?" I asked.

"Same as you, in Canada," he replied.

"I thought you were an American."

"Yeah, but lots of Americans were trained by the British in Canada. The British came to Texas in the winter of 1917-18."

"I heard about that," said Bill.

"Fools didn't know if they could fly in the Canadian winters," said Tom.

"If you can dress for bad weather on the ground, you can do it to fly too," I said.

"They found that out soon enough I guess," continued Tom.

"Were you with the group that flew in the Canada in the winter?"

"Yeah, last winter. I was with the boys who stayed in Canada when the rest of the Flying Corps went to Texas to enjoy the sun. We had to stay in Canada to experiment and to find out if we could continue training in the cold."

"What was it like? I remember that winter as being one of the hardest in a long time," said Bill.

"It was cold. I remember them telling us that it was one of the coldest winters on record. We were busy trying the new biplane skis. It wasn't that bad, I guess. We sure bundled up though."

"It probably prepared us for the cold out here on the front."

"That's right," said Tom. "I think one of the best things that happened to me was when I was in the *clink*."

"How did you get in there?"

"It was as easy as could be. I wasn't even trying to get into jail. I couldn't believe it when a real first class guy, an instructor, came up to me at the end of the day, when I was tired like everyone else, and told me to go back and drain the oil out of his biplane. We were draining our motors every night so that we could take the oil inside the hangars. It would be warm in the morning when it was time to pour it back into the motor. That warmed the motor enough to start it. Anyway, I told the guy that I didn't care what his rank was; everyone drained his own motor. I had done quite enough by that time. He seemed to realize that he was out of line and went and did it himself. The next day, I found out that he had reported it to the Commanding Officer. I was dragged to the door of the officer. Just as I was about to step into the C.O.'s office, a military police officer pulled my hat off and thrust it into my hand. I stood in front of the big man and the charges were read. He looked at me for a moment and said, 'seven days'."

"I guess you were happy," I said.

"I sure was. The *clink* was warm. There was nothing to do most of the time but rest. I remember that I had only been in the *clink* for a few days when a poor dog had been hit by a truck. I was given orders to bury it. I went out there with a MP and began my efforts to dig a hole. I worked for a couple of hours without success. I swear that it must have been granite that I was trying to chop through. Finally, the MP walked up and said, 'Look lad, there is nothing happening here. Let's get this sorry thing put away.' 'Sure,' I replied to him. We dragged the dog to a nearby snowdrift. We dug a fast hole in the snow and threw it in. That spring some of the boys in the *clink* must have really smelled it. I'm sure there were some around who knew what had happened."

"I remember another incident that occurred when I was at Camp Borden. The Americans in the camp were responsible for it," said Bill.

"I hope there is no dog in this story," I said.

"Yeah, I'm afraid there is a dog, but it fared much better. Of course, the Brits ran the Royal Flying Corps. The Camp I was at was the same way. The Commanding Officer was one of those real straight-laced *Brits*. He was a tall guy who did everything by the book. Life was one long set of rules to follow. Well, the Americans on the base were not interested in the rules. They used to say that if you wanted to just follow rules all day, then you should join the navy. They were there to fly—to get the war over with."

"All of the serious pilots are like that," said Tom.

"Well, this tall C.O. used to walk around camp with his huge Saint Bernard. The old guy expected everyone to salute him. He would look for anything that could be seen as an infraction of the rules. He found them too."

"It wouldn't take long for something to happen with him doing that," I said.

"That's right. I can't remember if it was because he charged someone in particular or because he was

102

generally hated, but one summer day his dog was kidnapped. The boys shaved the dog on one side and wrote the dog's name, BRUNO, on the shaved side with paint. The C.O. marched the animal through the camp. He never did find out who did it," said Bill.

"I wonder whether we got anything of value from our training," I said.

"They taught us to fly. What else did you expect?" asked Tom.

"To be honest, they really only taught us how to take off and how to land."

"Well, I don't know about that," said Bill.

"What else is there? After only a few hours of training, we could go up and come down safely. Then, all we did was get in the cockpit every morning and spend the day in the air flying, learning how to fly on our own."

"I thought that was the best part," said Bill.

"It was a good time. The real challenges and lessons came from the other guys we were flying with. I remember when we were training; the last test you had to pass before anyone would consider you a pilot was to chase a passenger train. The trains were on a regular schedule between the towns of Baxter and Ivy and the distance was perfect. What we had to do was fly in behind the train. The telephone poles were wide enough to allow us to fly over the train. Then, we would come right up to the roof level of the passenger car. As we would fly toward the front of the train, we would touch our wheels on each passenger car roof. Once we got to the front of the train, we would swoop down in front of the train and fly for a while. After we had done that, we had to pull up and to the right as fast as possible so that the engineer couldn't read the registration numbers on the side of the plane. No one ever got caught while I was there."

"We did that same kind of antic," said Tom.

"What did you do?"

"We had an iron works near by. We flew our biplanes through the uprights of the cranes in the yards. We had to fly into the yard, go through and pull up hard to clear the fence on the far side. When I was there, a guy who did it was so happy that he went right back for a second time. He must have been overconfident because he forgot that he only had one and half inches on each side. He crashed and never made it."

"That takes me back to what I was saying. Do we really get any training in the schools?" I asked.

"I think we did," said Bill. "We each had to fly by ourselves and find out what we could do. That is probably the best training you can get."

"If you're going to have any trouble flying, you would know it right away on those first lessons when the instructor goes with you. I remember one time a friend of mine, Bob, was at the controls for the first time. The instructor was in the back seat. Bob was hanging on to the stick hard, then he froze. The instructor tried to take control, but he couldn't. Something had to be done. The instructor, screaming at the top of his voice, had no effect. He grabbed a wrench and hit Bob across the head," said Tom.

"Was he okay after that?"

"Sure. He had his thick leather helmet on. He woke up before they landed. He now is an air mechanic," said Tom.

"I'm not surprised," I said.

"Those were some good days," said Bill. We looked at him and nodded in agreement. We listened to the distant shells. In the morning, we would be over the trenches again making observations and fighting off the enemy.

15. The Katherine Stinson Story

I'm Ken Wilson, reporter for the *Winnipeg Free Press*. In the spring of 1916, I was called into the editor's office. I sat down, unsure of what my assignment would be. I had asked several times if I could go to France to cover the war. I hoped that the editor, Ed Thomas, would give me that assignment, but somehow I knew he was going to ask me to do something else. After I stepped into his office, I stood watching him as he walked from the huge windows at the back of his office over to the desk, and then waved his hand toward the chair in front of his desk.

"I have an assignment for you Ken. It isn't the assignment that you have been hounding me about. I have no idea why you want to go to France and cover the war."

"It is the only big story," I assured him. He glared at me.

"That's true," he continued. "War, war, war, that's all we ever hear about. We have to know what is happening, but we need something else. People need some good news."

"I thought that was what you would ask me to do."

"If you really want to go to the front in France, you could always sign up as a soldier."

"Thanks, I would be more valuable as a correspondent."

"What I want you to do is the Katherine Stinson story."

"Who is she? Oh yes, I read that she is an American woman who flies a biplane at exhibitions. I wonder if she's any good."

"Well, you'll find out soon enough. She has quite a reputation for flying as good as any of the guys who flew before the war."

"Where is she flying?"

"She's going to start in Calgary, then go to Edmonton, Brandon, and Regina. She plans to finish here in Winnipeg to raise money for the patriotic fund. The stories that we print in advance of her arrival will help bring people out."

"You're supporting the patriotic fund? I thought you were on a crusade against the war?"

"Ken, you know better than that. Like everyone else, I am just tired of it."

"I'll be on my way."

"Good," said Ed.

I arrived in Calgary on June 29. Miss Stinson was to give a flying demonstration on the 30th. I found a ride to the exhibition grounds with a friend, Jack

Edwards, a reporter for the *Calgary Herald*. Jack heard that Stinson had arrived and that her mechanics were busy getting her machine ready. We saw the biplane as soon as we got there. We drove right up to it, then got out of the car to get a better look.

"Hello, can I help you?" asked a woman in overalls. Jack and I looked at the woman for a moment.

"I'm Ken Wilson from the *Winnipeg Free Press* and this is Jack from the *Calgary Herald.*"

"How do you do," she said.

"Are you Miss Stinson?" asked Jack.

"Yes, I'm Katherine," she said.

"Oh, well how do you do?" I said. "Will the machine be ready to fly tomorrow?" I asked.

"It's ready to fly now," she said.

"What are you planning to do tomorrow?" asked Jack.

"Just fly like I always do."

"What does that entail Miss Stinson," asked Jack.

"Well, I usually take off, do a few small stunts, then land."

"Do you have anything new to show the crowd in Calgary?"

"I think that the crowd will like my demonstration. It really isn't new, but it is fun. Would you like to go flying?" she asked Jack.

"No! I mean I don't think that would be proper."

"Oh, I want to take the biplane up to check how it's flying."

"Well, if you are going up anyway, I would be glad to join you," I said. Jack jabbed me in the ribs once. "I think it would be good for me to get some firsthand experience. It would help me with writing about your show."

"Splendid," she said. "Get in the back and put the harness on."

It was only moments before we were climbing in the air. The biplane ascended until we were above the clouds. We made easy turns to the left and to the right. Stinson climbed a little more, then pushed the stick forward and dove toward the ground. I couldn't believe the speed we were flying at. Then she pulled up hard and climbed until we were above the clouds again. In one easy motion, the biplane dove down again, twisted to the right, then to the left, and finished with a hard pull upwards.

Jack looked bewildered as I climbed out of the back cockpit.

"Thank you!" called Miss Stinson. "I enjoyed the ride."

"I should be the one to thank you. That was an impressive ride you gave me."

"Not at all," she said. "I have to go now," she continued with a wave of her hand. She walked into one of the nearby buildings of the exhibition grounds.

"Are you crazy?" asked Jack.

"What are you talking about?"

"I wouldn't fly on most days, but if I did decide to fly, I would have to see the pilot fly first."

"I don't think you have to worry about a pilot inviting you to fly and not knowing how to fly."

"I still think that was crazy," said Jack.

"Let's go to the café. I will try to talk you into going for a flight some day."

"Sure, let's do that," said Jack.

* * *

When I watched Miss Stinson flying the next day, she did a lot of good nosedives. She would dive downward and pull up in steep turns. There were steep spirals and loops.

Stinson was scheduled to do three flights a day. I ran to Jack's car in the parking lot of the exhibition grounds after the first demonstration. Jack agreed to let me use the typewriter at his office. He had also volunteered his telephone so that I could get my stories in. Jack was sitting on the bumper of the car waiting for me.

"What's the hurry?" asked Jack.

"She's flying two more times today. I want to make it back in time to see at least one of those flights."

"You're in a hurry just to see one more of her flights?"

"That's what I said."

"Well, you're not the only one who is impressed."

"I know. The crowd was really taken in by her flying."

"That's not what I meant. I was watching with some of my friends from Sarcee military camp. Well, they went right over there when she landed and invited her to their camp as an honored guest for dinner."

"That's great. I can use that in my story."

111

"We can go and write our stories, then we can go to the café," said Jack.

"No, I will want to come back."

"Ken, she is going to be flying for four more days."

"What if her biplane breaks down? That happens a lot you know."

"This is Stinson we are talking about. She has a record of making up flights she can't do. I checked on that this morning."

"I'm not surprised, but I have to come back for at least one more flight today."

"Ken, that's crazy."

"Sorry," I said.

"I think you are really taken by this lady," said Jack.

"Maybe I am taken with her flying."

"Okay, we can come back, but after that you owe me a supper," said Jack.

"All right, it is a deal."

We did go back that evening for her last flight. I think her flying was better the third time. She must have felt freer as the day went on.

* * *

Both Jack and I drove to Regina when Stinson was to do her show there.

"When we get to Regina, let's go straight to the exhibition grounds," I said.

"You just want to see if she is there, right?" said Jack.

"That's my assignment," I replied.

"Your job is not to hound her all the time. You don't have to be there for every flight she makes.

"I like this assignment. That's why I am doing a little extra work."

"You haven't even spoken to her since that day she gave you that ride."

"Does that matter?"

"Okay, we can go to the exhibition grounds."

Jack drove through the city with the hot summer sun beating down on us. Soon, we were at the grounds where people were busy putting up circus tents and booths for the fair. Jack drove along the side of the grounds slowly.

"Look, there she is," I said. I pointed across the field.

"Good, now we have seen that she is here. That is all you asked to see," said Jack.

"Yeah, you're right. Let's go to your brother's place," I said.

"I'm surprised," said Jack.

"Why?"

"I thought you would want to go over there and talk to her to see if you can get a ride," he said.

"No, I just wanted to see if she was here and to see where she was parked so that we can get there faster in the morning."

"Okay, that's fine," said Jack as he turned the car around and headed downtown again.

* * *

The next day, we arrived early. It was already hot, but the grass was still fresh. It had not yet been trampled down between the booths. The air was alive with the smell of popcorn and lemonade. I was glad that I had the Katherine Stinson assignment. It had turned into a nice summer holiday. I walked through the displays, and then went to where we had seen the biplane the day before. I watched the crowd push around the plane. I stepped closer and noticed that Stinson was among the crowd as if she was only one of the Regina citizens looking over the plane. She walked slowly around the biplane. I stepped up to the biplane looking at all the rigging.

I felt a hand on my shoulder. "Hello," said a familiar voice. I turned to see Stinson beside me.

"Hello, you're here too?"

"Well, yes, I am. The newspaper wants me to cover all you exhibitions," I said.

"Would you like to fly again with me?"

"Sure, Miss Stinson."

"Well, then you can come with me during the exhibition," she said.

Going up with her on a test flight was all right, but to go when she was actually putting on a show was different.

"Well, I don't know," I said.

"Last time I took you up, I did all the same maneuvers I do during my show. These biplanes can do more than what us pilots show you people at these exhibitions."

"I'll believe you, but I don't know anything about flying," I said.

"You get into the cockpit in the back and buckle up. I'll wait a moment, and then I will get into the front. Watch the look on the faces of all these people when I step from this crowd and get into the cockpit," she said.

As she climbed on to the wing moments after I had buckled myself into the seat, I noticed that a man put his hand out as though he was looking at a woman who was some place she was not supposed to be. He stopped himself only an inch away from Stinson. He slowly pulled his hand back and stared like the rest of the people in the crowd.

As we ascended above the clouds, then descended, I realized that Stinson was right. The ride was just like the one in Calgary except for the last dive. The pressure grew on my ears. I heard a hissing sound in my ears. They ached. Then as she turned the biplane downward, the pressure decreased. The dive began higher than the others and it was much faster. Stinson pushed the biplane as fast as she could toward the ground. We came in toward the ground, and then she pulled up hard and turned left. I never imagined that I could go from feeling completely weightless, as I did when we were high above the clouds, to that excited giddy feeling I had during the dive. When we pulled up, I felt heavier than ever before. The biplane lifted and circled gently above the field. Without any more maneuvers, we landed. The crowd applauded.

Stinson turned and asked, "Where are you from?"

My ears hurt and I could barely hear her.

"Winnipeg," I replied.

"Good, I'll have something special for that show," she said.

"Thank you again."

"I must be going," she said. Stinson stepped out of the cockpit and into the crowd.

I found out later that several people had phoned the police to ask if there had been an accident. They were sure that with such a steep dive, the biplane had crashed.

I left the exhibition grounds. I followed Stinson to Brandon, where she flew the same stunts she has flown to that point.

I waited with anticipation for the show in my hometown.

Stinson's flight at Winnipeg was scheduled for August 3, but her biplane was damaged in a storm before the fair opened. We all stood around and watched as Stinson's mechanics worked. The day passed into the evening. It was 10:30 PM by the time it was ready. The fair grounds were still full of people. The organizers called for a number of cars to be lined up along the field where Stinson would have to land. With the car's headlights on, she could see where the landing area was.

She was going to fly, they said. I was surprised and excited. If anyone could fly at night and in the dark, she could. There was one problem. How would anyone see her?

Before I could even think about it, I heard the loud roar of the motor. In a moment, Stinson was in the air. I watched as he plane disappeared in the darkness above us. We could only hear her biplane's motor.

Then it was as though the sky was on fire; the biplane had been rigged with flares on the wings and tail.

The next day, she carried on with an incredible show. A paper castle was built overnight. The show included a castle and a whole corps of soldiers who were firing rifles with blanks. The soldiers pounded the sky with their rifles as Stinson bombed that paper castle.

I never saw Katherine Stinson after that. I also never saw a flying demonstration better than I had seen that summer.

16. Law in the Sky

What I remember the most from the First World War has little to do with my experience in the Royal Flying Corps. It happened in the summer of 1917 when I was training for the Royal Flying Corps. A short woman named Ruth Law gave a flying demonstration. She flew on June 29. Everyone was talking about her around the training camp before she arrived.

"I swear we will see something new from her if we go to the exhibition," Sam, one of our fellow flying mates, insisted.

"You say you saw her fly in the United States when you didn't know anything about flying, right?" I said.

"Yes, that's right," he replied.

"Well, no matter what you saw her do, you would have been impressed."

"No, not at all," said Stan.

"You still think she will show us something we haven't seen?" said Fred, who had been sitting quietly at the table listening.

"Yes."

"I can't agree. We fly everyday. We try everything we can in order to learn how to fly. You want us to believe that this flying lady has more experience?" I asked.

"She has been flying since 1912."

"Why does that matter?"

"We have only a few months of experience on our own." said Stan.

"But we do more because we're training to go to war."

"We can settle this fast," said Stan.

"How?"

"We can go see her fly."

"When is she flying?"

"On the twenty-ninth."

"I can't go," I said.

"Why?"

"That's the same day as the car racing show."

"Then you will be there," said Stan. "That is where she is going to be flying."

"Is she going to race the cars?"

"Yes. She gives the cars a head start, then flies right on top of them."

"What's new about that? We do that everyday. Yesterday, I dropped my wheels on the roof of a bus. The driver nearly had a heart attack. He almost drove into the ditch. I think I'd better just do that to trains; the tracks keep them straight," I said.

120

"You'll see what else she does," said Stan. We got up from the dinner table, and then went back to the barracks for the night.

* * *

It was a beautiful summer day when we all gathered outside the gate of the Royal Flying School to go to the car races and see Law fly. All of us had the day off. The grass looked greener than I had seen it all year. I couldn't wait to get to the exhibition.

"Hey Stan, what kind of plane does this lady fly anyway?" I asked as we climbed into a 1914 McLaughlin.

"I'm pretty sure she has one of those old Curtiss biplanes," he replied.

"You mean one of those old pusher type biplanes?" asked Fred.

"That's right," replied Stan.

"Why is she still flying that kind of machine?"

"Probably because it was cheap. You can also pull it apart and ship it in a crate on the train."

"Well, I'll give her credit for taking one of those old clunky biplanes into the air," I said.

"That's true," agreed Fred.

The breezes that flowed into the open windows of the McLaughlin made me feel refreshed. We had nothing to do but go to the races and enjoy ourselves.

Soon, we were close to the exhibition grounds. There were crowds of people moving around the racing cars and the biplane.

"Hey, let's get over to the biplane and take a look," I said.

"Sure," said Stan as he continued to drive until we were close to the machine. In a few moments, we were out of the car and walking around the biplane.

"It's a Curtiss all right," said Fred.

"But, it doesn't look right to me," said Stan.

"What do you mean?" asked Fred.

"I'm not sure," said Stan. He stood staring at the front of the craft.

"You're right. Those aren't the right controls," I said. "The Curtiss biplanes have a steering wheel on the top of the control stick. This is wrong. There are two sticks on this machine; one on each side of the pilot's seat."

"Fred, what do you make of it?" asked Stan.

"I've seen controls like that before," he said. He stared for a moment thinking about it. "I know what it is. Those are from the Wright Brother's Company."

"That's right," I said. "I wonder why she has her machine set up like this?"

"Because I had to," came a voice from behind us. We turned and looked at the small woman walking toward us.

"Miss Law?" I asked.

"Yes, I am," she replied.

"What do you mean you had to put those controls on the Curtiss biplane?"

"Well, when it came time for me to buy a biplane, I went to the Curtiss Company in New York. The company refused to sell me a machine. I waited for a second hand machine to come my way. The only problem was that the controls that were on it did not work. I found a set of Wright controls and had them installed. They work fine."

"Why didn't Curtiss sell you a biplane?" asked Stan.

"I told you what I know. You can guess as well as anyone what the company's reason was," she said.

"Well, I don't know if I would fly a machine like this one," I said.

"It's a part of the show, I guess," she said. "You boys are flying with the RFC, right?"

"Yes," said Stan.

"That is where all the good biplanes go. I would really like one of the Jennies you fly."

"They can do a lot," said Fred.

"Well, I have to get this engine oiled and going. I have to race soon and I would like to try out this motor first," said Miss Law. She turned away from us and pulled an oilcan out of her toolbox. She moved over to the engine and went to work.

"Would you like some help?" asked Stan.

"No, I do this all the time. I should do it myself because I know what this motor needs. You guys go enjoy the rest of the show."

"Okay, we'll see you later," I said as we walked to the cars. I can barely remember any of the cars at all. All I can remember is anticipating seeing Law fly that pusher biplane.

Finally, the time came. We sat down in the grandstands ready to watch the race. She had to race against a Gaston Chevrolet. The Chevy had to race to only five laps of the track and Law had to fly six laps.

123

She came in on the track low to reduce the distance. The car was moving at top speed down the straightaway, but it had to slow down a little on the corners. For Law, the corners were not as easy. She couldn't slow down and she couldn't turn too tight either. She pulled up high and had to swing wide around the outside of the track. She had to stay that wide for the rest of the race. Law had to cover so much extra distance that it was not surprising when she lost the race by about a third of the track's length. The real exciting flying was about to begin.

After a short stop, the small pusher biplane climbed into the air to give the flying exhibition we had all waited for. She climbed in a smooth circle above our heads. Once she had gained enough height, she flattened out and completed an even loop.

"Not much happening yet," said Fred.

"She hasn't even begun to show us what she can do," said Stan.

We listened to the distant hum of the small motor as she completed her loop. Fred was wrong when he said that nothing had happened. We had just started learning how to loop and really couldn't do it well yet. She had flattened out, continued to pull the biplane up, and then did a number of vertical turns. The motor roared as she completed the turns. Then, she pointed the nose of the aircraft to earth and dived. The crowd was silent. We were all unsure that she would have the strength to pull the biplane back up.

Of course, she did pull up at the last moment, and climb to the height she had been at before. Again, we watched as she pointed the nose of her aircraft to the ground.

"Is that all we are going to see? Climbs and dives?" asked Fred.

No one answered. We were a little uncomfortable at the aggressive way Law was able to fly her biplane. We sat straight up, feeling sick to our stomachs. The small biplane began to spin. At that time, we only knew that once you had made a mistake and went into a spin, you couldn't do anything except crash. We had heard rumors that someone in Britain had figured out a way to recover from a spin, but no one in Canada knew whether it was just a rumor or whether it could actually be done. We stared in disbelief as the wings stopped spinning. Law was in a simple dive. Like the first dive, she pulled up and continued to climb back to the height she had been at. Again, the pusher biplane nosed toward the earth and began to spin. We all stared with the same fear that had filled us moments earlier. She repeated her recovery. In a few moments, she landed safely. The crowd stood up.

My friends and I stood up more slowly than the rest of the audience. No one said anything. We had one goal in mind as we left the stands. We had to know how she stopped spinning. We made our way to where the large crowd had gathered. Law was gone. No one knew where she went or if she would be back.

As it turned out, she was gone for the day. We never saw her again. Even though we had seen the recovery from the spin, we couldn't tell anyone about it at the school. We would have been laughed at. Even though was had seen it twice, it had happened so fast that we had no idea how it was done. None of us were ready to experiment with a spin in those days.

They had discovered how to recover from a spin in England. We all found out about it when we arrived there. The schools began teaching it right after we left. Too bad pilots didn't know how to stop a spin earlier. A lot of crashes could have been avoided.

As for Law, when we got back to the school, her performance was all we could talk to each other about for days.

17. Canada's First Air Mail With a Stunt in Montreal

They always said that to be a good pilot during the First World War you needed to have *dash* and be resourceful. Right, well here I am in the training school in Toronto without any way to see how much dash I had. I have been here too long to enjoy it. The year, 1918, is just six months old, but I feel like it is already 1919. I want to go home this weekend. Montreal is the place for me. The only questions are how am I going to get the time off to go there? How can I get an airplane to get there? I considered just taking one and doing what I wanted, but I knew that wouldn't be possible. They would notice the plane missing in a moment. I thought about the problem for a while, and then came up with a long shot idea. I guess you could say I had the *dash* to figure it out.

I marched confidently up to the office of the headman of the Royal Air Force training school. The man I was about to speak to was Brigadier General Hoare. I stepped past the Military Police who guarded his door and knocked loudly.

"Come," came the stern call from the other side of the door. I opened the door and stepped in.

"Sir," I said and saluted.

"Captain Brian Peck, to what do I owe the honor by your visit?"

"I have to speak to you about an important issue that has come up, sir."

"What is it about?" he asked.

"New recruits, sir."

"Is there a problem with one of our new boys?"

"No sir."

"Then, what is the issue?"

"I have an idea to bring in more recruits, sir."

"At ease, Brian. We want to get all the new boys in here that we can. What is your idea?"

"It is simple and straightforward."

"Then let's hear it."

"The largest numbers of young boys out there are from the cities."

"Of course—"

"We need to show them why they should join the RFC."

"Brian, what is did you have in mind?"

"A simple demonstration of flying to the city boys. Show them in real terms what it is like to fly. Make them want to fly."

"A flying demonstration for city lads? I presume that it would be at the summer fairs."

"No sir. We cannot wait for the summer fairs. We should get right out there and show the lads on the streets what we can do. We have to fly into the cities and show the boys and anyone else who watches what flying is all about."

"Flying over some cities and doing stunts? Put on a real show?" he asked.

"I suggest that such an effort would demonstrate in simple terms why they should serve."

"Really Brian?"

"Most of the boys we get here now are here because they saw a biplane fly once and wanted to try it themselves. If they just wanted to serve in the war, they would have joined the army long ago."

"I think you may have something. The lads need to be drawn into the Royal Flying Corps."

"Yes sir," I said.

"Tell me, Brian, when do you think these demonstrations should begin?"

"No more time should be lost. I believe that we should begin immediately."

"Tomorrow?"

"Oh, no. Not that soon. I would say that the best time would be this weekend."

"Why on the weekend?"

"Oh, I figure that many people work indoors on the week days. Others are in school."

"School lads would be underage."

"I mean strictly college lads, sir."

"I see. Tell me Brian, what city would we begin with? Maybe Toronto because it is close?"

"No sir."

"Oh? Why not?"

"Well the lads of Toronto live so close that they have had the opportunity to see flying whenever they want to see. No, sir, I would suggest Montreal first."

"You are suggesting a flight to Montreal this weekend to give a demonstration over the streets of that city."

"Yes, sir. That flight would be the beginning of our recruitment campaign."

"Brian, would the fact that you are from Montreal have anything to do with your plan?" asked Hoare with a smile.

"Absolutely not, sir," I replied.

"No, I didn't think so. I do like the idea. Everyone knows that we need more recruits if we want to bring this war to a close. Yes, I would suggest you follow up on this plan."

"Yes, sir. I shall carry out the plan with as much speed as I can."

"Oh Brian," said Hoare. "Do have a good weekend."

"Yes sir," I replied. I turned and stepped out of the office. I felt good as I walked across the grounds to the instruction hall.

* * *

As I sat down at a table, Corporal Mathers sat down beside me.

"Brian, what has happened to you today? You look like you won all the card games last night," he said.

"It was something like that. You remember that I was talking about not being able to get out of here enough?" I said.

"Right, you have been carrying on about going to Montreal if only you had half the chance."

"I got my wish."

"How did you do that?"

"I went right into see the top man and made a little proposal that he liked right away," I said.

"May I ask what this proposal was?" asked Mathers.

"I pointed out that we needed some new recruits and that the best way to get more lads interested was to show them how great flying really was."

"Tell me how you proposed to get this new interest in the lads of this far flung country."

"Not just any lads, Mathers, I wanted the city boys to be sold on the idea of joining the RFC to fly."

"Well, I can see it now. You wanted to get recruits from Montreal. You had a reason to go there. Now, tell me how you are going to make the boys want to come to the RFC?"

"I suggested that I fly over the city and give a flying demonstration to the lads in the streets."

"And he bought the idea?"

"With a little work on my behalf, he appreciated it."

"When are you going to give this demonstration?"

"This weekend," I said.

"I'll be—" he said. "You know I have a forty-eight hour leave this weekend; how about if I come along?" asked Mathers.

"You realize this is all the most serious of business," I said.

"Oh, of course," Mathers agreed.

"Well, then you are counted in on this venture."

"Thanks, I will be packed in no time. I have to go to the store to pick up a few things. Do you want to come along?" asked Mathers.

"Sure."

In a few moments, we had made our way to the store.

"Good day," said Mathers to the man who ran the store.

"Hello," he replied.

"We are in for a few items before we go on our leave," I said.

"Where are you guys going for your leave?"

"Montreal," replied Mathers.

"How are you getting there? You could only make it there and back if you had one of our planes," said the storekeeper.

"That's what we're are going to do. We get a biplane because we are going to be doing some RFC business while we are there," I said.

"You're lucky," he said. "I was hoping to get to Quebec in the near future, but I don't think I will be able to."

"Why Quebec?" asked Mathers.

"I am getting married. I wanted to get something suitable for the celebration. Ontario has nothing at all these days," he said.

"I do believe we can be of service to you," I said.

"Really?"

"Of course. We can pick up a crate of what I think you need," I said.

"Thank you. How much do you think it will cost?"

"We will consider it a gift for the big day," said Mathers.

"Thank you," replied the storekeeper, smiling.

Early in the morning on June twentieth, Mathers and I walked out of the barracks prepared for our weekend trip to Montreal. There was a cool breeze. The sky was dark with clouds.

"Well Mathers, it is best to get up there before the clouds get the better of us," I said.

"That sounds like a good idea to me. I don't want to give up a weekend in the city for anything," said Mathers.

"That's my view too."

We climbed into the cockpit and prepared to take off. We could see that cool breeze was more like a hard wind. The clouds weren't harmless either. We had to get above them and push a course through to Montreal as fast as we could.

As I pulled the plane up into the air, I knew we had to watch the wind that was coming from the south. When we got as far as Deseronto, we had to land to get more fuel because we were flying against the wind.

Of course, in 1918 there were not many landing fields like there are today. When you were getting ready to fly anywhere, you had to make arrangements with farmers or golf courses to land your biplane. In Montreal, we had contacted the Officer Commanding Military District No. 4 to land at the Bois Franc Polo Grounds. I was hungry, cold and tired as I circle above the Polo Grounds that afternoon. The bad weather did not end at all as we flew to Montreal. The area was clear. I circled one more time and came in for a landing.

As we bumped along the Polo field, I noticed a small collection of men waiting. The one in uniform was obviously the Commander of the Military District, but the other two were in civilian clothes. I taxied the biplane close to the small group and turned the motor off.

Mathers got out of his cockpit and saluted the commander as I stepped down from the biplane. I saluted the commander as he began to speak.

"Glad you're here. I will have the biplane placed under guard."

"Thank you, sir. Thank you for arranging this landing field for us," I said.

"You are welcome," he replied.

"Hello," said one of the two men who stood nearby.

"Hello, I am Brian Peck," I said.

"We know. This is Edmund Greenwood," said the man. "And I am George Lighthall, the president of the Montreal branch of the Aerial League of the British Empire. Edmund is the treasurer."

"Well, this is a pleasure," I said.

"We were happy to hear that you were arriving to carry out flying demonstrations in our city. We have another idea of what you could do while you are here," continued George.

"What is that?"

"For some time we have thought it would be good to start having mail moved by plane instead of train. We would like you to carry a package of mail with you back to Toronto. It would be the first official air mail sent in Canada."

"That does sound like a good idea," I agreed. George smiled widely at Edmund.

"Well, what arrangements have to be made?"

"Don't worry. We will call the postal officials in Ottawa and prepare the mail for you."

"That sounds fine to me. I can meet you back here tomorrow. I am hoping to carry out my first flight for the city then."

"That sounds fine," replied Greenwood.

With the biplane under guard, Mathers and I set out for the city to enjoy ourselves.

* * *

The next day, the weather did not improve. It was raining and a wind was blowing. Mathers and I walked slowly around our biplane. Soon, we noticed the two men from the day before walking toward us.

"Hello, George," I said.

"Good day," he replied.

"Do you think the rain is going to stop?"

"No. I'm afraid the forecast is bad."

"How are things going with the post office?" asked Mathers.

"We contacted the post office officials in Ottawa. I was made a post-master for the event. We will be

135

receiving about one hundred and twenty letters for the trip to Toronto on Monday."

"That sounds good to us," Mathers said.

"We will have them stamped and delivered soon."

"I guess there will be no flying today," I said.

"No, it doesn't look like it," replied George. "Do you men have any plans?"

"No," replied Mathers.

"Why don't you come with us? We know an excellent restaurant," said George.

"That sound good," said Mathers.

The same weather prevailed on Sunday. We did not stay around the biplane that long. It was clear that we would not be able to take off. Monday dawned with bad weather as well, but Mathers and myself decided we would try to take off. Not only were there clouds and drizzle, but also the clouds were quickly dropping in altitude. We moved fast to get the biplane off the ground. The mail we were given was marked June 23, 1918. It had to get off the ground that day. The mail did get *off the ground*, but that was all. I had to circle and come right down to the ground again because of the fog. We had to wait until June 24 before weather cleared enough to take off. We filled the fuel tank right up so that we could get all the way to Toronto. Added to the weight was the entire crate of "Old Mull" for the storekeeper's wedding and Mathers in the back. The biplane was too heavy to climb very fast.

I pushed forward on the throttle and made the motor roar with all the fuel I could give it. Right in front of me and at the side of the Polo Grounds was a telegraph wire. I could see that I was climbing too slowly to clear the wire. I noticed right away that there were a lot of wires right behind the cable I had just flown under. I pushed hard to turn the biplane and follow straight down the railway tracks. I was only a few feet above the tracks and ahead I noticed that there was a bridge coming at me very fast. Because there were wires all over the place, I continued to fly toward the bridge. I banked as hard as I could without risking a stall and just missed the bridge. Finally, I was over the water and in the clear. I had the room now to climb slowly to a good flying level. I continued until I came to the lake at Two Mountains. After five miles, I had climbed forty feet and was able to turn overland toward Toronto.

The situation didn't get any better. We flew with a strong west wind and heavy rain that came in squalls. I was just feeling comfortable when a fuel line plugged and the motor sputtered. I felt sick with the possibility of a forced landing. It meant losing all the height I had gained. It looked like the flight was about to end for the day. I prepared to start dropping the nose of the biplane when the motor began to hum continuously. I continued to fly on to Kingston.

As we reached the city, the fuel gage indicated that the tank was empty. I did not know if anyone in the city had the right kind of fuel, but we didn't have any choice. The biplane came down and landed. Because no one had any high-grade fuel, we had to settle for regular automobile fuel. We accepted only half a tank.

As the motor turned, I was not sure if I would get off the ground. The motor fired on every second cylinder only. I opened the throttle wide and added a little extra choke. We held on and climbed slowly moving to our next destination of Deseronto. We knew we could get the proper fuel there. When we got there, we drained out the car fuel, put in aircraft fuel and took off. We arrived in Toronto after 4 PM and the bag of letters just made it into the post office in time. I handed the bag to Post Master W.E. Lemon at 4:55 PM

"We weren't sure that you would make it today," said Lemon.

"We weren't sure either but here is the mail," I said,

"I wish we had something to give you for the effort."

"Don't worry about that," I said.

"I know what we can give you," said Lemon as he turned the bag of mail upside down pouring the letters into a wood hopper in the Post Office.

"Here take the bag as a souvenir."

"Well, thank you. This bag might be worth something some day," I said.

"I hope so," said the postmaster.

"Well, we have to get the biplane back to the Leaside School," I said.

"We have another delivery too," said Mathers.

Indeed we did. The storekeeper eagerly waited for the "Old Mull". He was getting married in a few days. He was probably more anxious than Post Master Lemon had been.

18. First Flight Across the Atlantic

Before the First World War broke out in 1914, many of us pilots dreamed of flying across the Atlantic. Probably one of us could have made it in short order, but the coming of the war meant that the effort stopped.

The experience of the War forced us to learn the physical elements of flight. Better flying machines were built too. With the war over, us pilots were certain that we could do anything. We were all going to find out what else the biplane could do. What kind of services could it bring to the public? Questions of how far we could go still pushed us forward. I wanted to know whether a biplane could fly non-stop across the Atlantic Ocean.

That was what John Alcock and I, Arthur Brown wanted to prove to ourselves in 1919. Yet, there were other factors that helped us. First, we found out that there were several other groups working at crossing the

Atlantic. We wanted to get there first. Flying across after someone else had just made it wouldn't be nearly as good. The second reason to get going was that Lord Northcliffe, who was the owner of the London *Daily Mail*, offered a prize of £10,000 to the first crew that made it across. With all that motivating us, we worked as fast as we could.

Both John Alcock and I were airmen during the First World War. Both of us had been shot down and became Prisoners of War. Officials at the Vickers Company who were going to supply the Vickers Vimy bomber for the flight asked me if I would partner with him for the effort to cross the Atlantic.

I remember we thought everything was lost about one month before we were prepared to take off from Newfoundland. We heard two crews were already on their way to England by plane.

But then the situation changed as fast as it had appeared to end for us.

"Hey, John we don't have to worry about those two crews that were organizing to take the Atlantic," I said. The date was May 27, 1919.

"Why? Did they call it off because it was too early in the year?"

"No they tried and didn't make it," I said with relief.

"Oh? What happened?"

"Well the first group, what was their names?"

"Grieve and Hawker?" said John.

"That's right. They took off, and then when everyone thought the crew had been lost at sea, they showed up on a Danish ship. They were taken to England. I think they ran out of fuel."

"What about those other two?"

"They had a bad field to take off from. They never made it off the ground."

"We still have a chance at making that first flight, but we have to hurry because there is no way of telling how long we will have before more people try."

"I couldn't agree with you more," I said. "Those boys who have that Hanley-Page Bomber are serious about going over too."

"I think that if they can get that huge pig of a biplane off the ground, it will probably stay up in the sky until the propellers pull it across."

We decided it was time to get our airplane into shape as fast as we could. We simply had to make it into the air to have a good chance at that crossing. The next day we arrived at a field near Quidi Vidi in Newfoundland. We wasted no time in setting to work on assembling the biplane. We had the biplane assembled on June 9th.

The *Vickers Vimy* had the military equipment stripped off of it. We added fuel tanks to carry 856 gallons, enough to allow us to fly 20 hours. Added to this we had two new Rolls Royce VIII engines that each had 360-horse power.

"I don't know, John," I said as we pulled ourselves out of the biplane after our first test flight. "The field is really bad."

"It is a little too short and uneven," replied John.

"Do you think we should even make an attempt at taking off with a full load?" I said.

"No, I don't think so. I really don't think we should take any unnecessary risks."

"The machine sounds fine to me."

"No problem with that. I think we better start looking for another field this afternoon," said John.

"There is another field that isn't too far away. We can go over there to make arrangements to take off from there right now," I said.

"Good," said John as he turned from the biplane. It didn't take long before we had a new field. We had the *Vickers Vimy* moved over to the new site that evening.

On June 12, 1919, we tested the biplane one more time. More importantly, we tested the field with a takeoff and a landing. With the successful test, we were ready to start loading our supplies. We prepared until the afternoon of June 14th.

We were working on the aircraft's motor when we heard a small voice call out to us.

"Hey boys, are you the ones that are going to fly across the Atlantic?" he asked.

"We are," said John.

"I'm the postmaster here. I have come to wish you good luck."

"Thank you very much," said John.

"I have a small request to make of you," said the man.

"What would that be?" I asked.

"I think it would be a good idea if you boys would take a bag of mail for England with you. I see it as a good luck charm."

John looked at me and smiled. "Well, I figure that sounds like a good idea," said John. Both of us probably had more faith in our toy cat mascot we were bring along.

"That's appreciated. I will have a special ink stamp made up. I'll get the bag to you by the time you are ready to go."

"Can you get it to us this afternoon?"

"I certainly can, and thank you," said the man as he turned and rushed across the field.

True to his word, he returned that afternoon with a small postal bag. We accepted it and packed it in the airplane.

* * *

That morning, we had received weather reports for the coast of Newfoundland and for the coast of England. Everything was clear. Because the Atlantic was known for having erratic weather, we couldn't be sure that the weather was really good all the way. All we were hoping was that with good weather reported on both sides, we might be able to reduce the chances of running into bad weather.

We got into the cockpit and were in the air at a few minutes to 2 o'clock.

Everything was perfect as the *Vickers Vimy* bounced down the field and rose into the air. I sat back in the seat and thought about how well everything had gone. Was this trip really going to be that easy? I hoped it would be. Maybe the other two crews that had tried earlier just had exceptionally bad luck. However, it was only a few hours into the flight when I became unsure about getting across.

143

I was awakened by the sound of a distant bang. At that same moment, the earpiece for the radio that I had been listening to went dead. I sat up high in the cockpit and looked out over the wing to the place where the small propeller driven generator had been rigged to run the radio. The propeller on the generator had broken off. The radio was no longer working. I remembered the story of Grieve and Hawker. They had experienced the same problem with their radio. Only hours after they took off, their radio went dead. No one heard anything from them for the rest of their trip.

I decided that I wouldn't tell John that the propeller took out an important support cable on the wing when it broke away.

I hardly had a chance to think about the two unfortunate men who had gone before us, when I saw a great mass of black clouds ahead. We had to climb to avoid the clouds, but soon realized that the climb would cost us too much fuel. We did not know how high such clouds could form. We just had to hold our pace through the thick fog and hope for the best. Soon, the sky turned dark as night approached.

Everything became a distant gray hum as the darkness of the night and fog, mixed with the roar of the wind. The biplane was being knocked around in the sky continuously, but we were able to keep our course. When we were both used to the rhythms of the flight, we did not expect anything abnormal.

I have no idea of how it happened, but the biplane's nose was knocked upward and stalled in the turbulence we were flying through. We were plunged into a full spin straight down to the dark ocean below.

144

As we spun downward, everything slowed down and I wondered if the fog would go on forever as it seemed to be while we flew on. It was entirely up to Alcock to pull us out of this. The spin stopped, but we were still plunging down. Slowly, the nose began to pull up. We hadn't leveled off as we broke through the fog. I could see the black inky ocean just below. As we leveled off, I imagined that we were like a stone that was skipping across the surface of the water.

As the nose of the airplane slowly began to rise, we could see that the dark ceiling of fog would envelop us in moments. The horizon disappeared. Alcock continued to pull up. A few moments later, we realized that we had pulled up too hard and the *Vickers Vimy* was just about to complete a loop the loop. Alcock struggled and leveled the aircraft out.

My job was to navigate, but I could not do anything for most of the journey, because the fog and the sleet obscured the world around us while we flew. Suddenly, the fog was gone. I quickly looked around, sighted the star Vega and took a reading. I checked the course we were flying and wrote it down. I handed the paper to Alcock. Soon, we were flying blind through the fog again.

I felt relief when we passed the Irish coast at 8:25 AM. We flew on, but we only found heavy low cloud as we approached what we thought was the English coast.

We searched for a level field to land on.

We began our descent. We could see the expanse of the field below us.

We dropped the last few feet to the ground. We touched lightly. Then, the gear took the full weight of the biplane. We were jerked hard as the landing gear pushed into the ground. The field was a soft bog. The gear crushed under us and the nose-dove into the bog. The front edge of the wings pushed close to the ground.

The abrupt end of the flight left us both feeling shocked. Alcock was all right, but I hit my face on the panel in front of me and had a few slight injuries. We had actually made it across the Atlantic. We landed near Cliveden at 8:40 AM, June 15, 1919. We had flown for sixteen hours and twelve minutes over a distance of about 1,800 air miles.

I can't remember too much about what I felt like after we landed. I know that both of us didn't get out of the *Vimy* for some time. We both were disoriented, deaf and dazed.

Both of us were helped out of the aircraft by the staff of the famous Marconi wireless station, which was about a mile away from our landing sight. We walked the short distance to the station with assistance.

We stayed for a day at the Marconi station and recovered. The next day we wired news of our success.

* * *

We expected to get the £10,000 for being the first across the ocean and maybe a party, be we did not expect to be given an audience with King George V at Buckingham Palace. We expected only to be congratulated. This was not what the King had planned. We were brought forward. Before we really knew what was happening, the ceremony was under way to give us knighthoods.

* * *

Long after the flight, I found that there was a story published that said that as we flew over the Atlantic Ocean, I got out of my seat and walked the wings of the *Vickers Vimy* to chip ice off the front of the engines, or off parts of the wing. If this actually happened, it would have been an even greater feat because when I was shot down during the First World War, my leg was injured. I never walked too well after that. According to one of those stories I walked out, during a sleet storm to chip ice off the front of an engine with a jack knife!

These stories may have been creative exaggerations of an incident that did happen. After we were coated with a thin layer of ice from sleet, I did have to unbuckle myself and straighten up to reach a fuel gage. I chipped a little ice away from the gage.

I guess a story about reaching out and chipping a little ice off a fuel gage isn't as exciting as walking out on an ice-covered wing to chip away at an engine with a jack knife.

19. The First Parachute: Jump With a Prayer

I'm Frank Ellis. When I think of the days when I was flying during the First World War for the Royal Flying Corps and later for the Royal Air Force, I am struck by how little we knew about flying. We did not know how to get out of a spin until 1918. Before that, any fighter pilot who got into a spin had no choice but to crash. Crashing with the machine was really the only option because we didn't have parachutes. Packed parachutes hadn't been invented or tested yet!

I always think about that because I was one of the first people to test a packed parachute at the end of the war. We were testing the first packed silk parachutes ever invented. Now, others had used parachutes in the earlier days of balloon flight, but there was only one man who had parachuted from an airplane. He had dared to try it in Vancouver a year earlier with an old bulky unpacked parachute that had been used on balloons. These parachutes were too bulky for biplanes.

Before I can tell you my story about parachuting, I should tell you how I got into a position where I could take that jump. Near the end of the war, the men of the Royal Air Force were told that they were to be discharged but that more staff was needed for the discharge office. With that announcement came a call for men to volunteer to work at the discharge office. I volunteered and was sent to Toronto. I was working in the office when I ran into Don Russell, an old friend who was a fighter pilot.

"Don, how's it going?" I asked as we shook hands.

"Not bad at all," he replied.

"What are you doing here? Are you trying to sign up?" I joked.

"No, I'm here like everyone else, trying to get the paper work done for my discharge."

"It will take time as usual. What are you going to be doing after you are discharged?"

"I have plans to build my own flying company."

"There will be a lot of men doing that with all these Curtiss Jenny training biplanes for sale for nearly nothing," I said.

"I figure I can make a real go of it," he said.

"Are you going to be one those who go to all the fairs and do demonstrations in summer?"

"That's from the past, Frank. I can see that the airplane is going to be a mode of transport in the future."

"I don't know about that."

"There is no question about it in my mind. We will be flying people and goods all over the country. The world has seen how important airplanes were in the war. People are ready to accept the air transport in their everyday lives."

"What is your company going to be doing?"

"My uncle owns most of it. He bought two Jennies. We are going to take the machines to Crystal beach resort and offer the people there a ride for a dollar a minute. We have another pilot, but we need a good airplane mechanic for our company."

"Well, you don't have to look any further because I would be happy to take the job."

"That's great. Are you putting through your own discharge right now?"

"No, but I can have a discharge in a week," I said.

"You can get your discharge that fast?"

"I work here, don't I? It can be done fast," I said. It was just under a week when I received my own papers for discharge. I was on my way to my new job with Don's *Allied Aeroplanes Limited*.

Since the Jennies weren't assembled when they were bought, the first job I had to do was put the two machines together. Once that job was completed, the biplanes had to be painted royal blue to cover the RAF colors.

On July 1, 1919, we were on our way to the resort on Lake Erie. The business did not go well at first. The pilot Don had hired crashed his biplane on the second landing.

Whenever we didn't have a passenger, we had to promote our company. The best way we had to do that

151

was to fly in low over the beach at the resort. We would fly along the sand and watch the tourists run for the beach houses or for the water. A few laid low and waited for us to pass.

There was only one way we could fly, directly at the huge concrete pier. At the moment everyone below thought a crash was inevitable, the biplane would pull up hard and clear the top of it.

Doing such stunts was the rule, not the exception for flying that summer. The reason was simple: the government had not thought about aircraft that much yet. Because airplanes were new, there were no regulations restricting flights or stunts dangerous to the public until 1923.

We were excited and ready to try anything when we flew out to the beach the first time on July 1, 1919. The sun was hot and the breeze was cool. With the First World War over, anything was possible. When the American inventor Leslie Irving contacted Don to test a packed parachute, we were excited. The offer could not be turned down. Irvin arrived. We were ready for our first parachute test on July 4th. The first volunteer to try the "chute" was another one of our American friends, Chelson.

That morning, Irvin, Chelson, Don and myself prepared for that first parachute jump near the beach on Lake Erie.

"Hey Leslie, why aren't you going to try this parachute out yourself?" asked Chelson.

"I did try it," he said as he limped to the small pile of equipment near the Jenny.

"When?" asked Don.

152

"Yesterday. That is how I got this sprained ankle. I jumped from a balloon and landed on the ground. I am going to have to figure out how to land on the ground after I'm finished testing this 'chute,'" he said.

"That's why you had me put on this bathing suit," said Chelson. "You want to drop me over the lake. I really can't swim that well, you know."

"That's what these are for," I said as I picked up the two inner tubes from the pile of things that had been brought for the jump.

"These will help you float and keep you from going too deep in the water," said Don.

"Right, these tires will probably mark the place where I was last seen," said Chelson.

"No, not at all," said Leslie. "We have everything worked out so that you will not fall out of the parachute or the tubes."

"How long will I be bobbing up and down in the water?" asked Chelson.

"Not long; we hired a boat and a crew. They will be on the lake and get there as fast as they can," said Don.

"Well let's get going. I want to try this out as soon as I can," said Chelson. He picked up the large packed parachute. "This is the way of the future? I have lifted loads of bricks that were lighter."

"Don't worry," said Irvin. He moved behind Chelson and adjusted the three huge belts in the front and back and clipped the heavy buckles closed. He finished by tightening each belt one more time.

"Well, let's get you into the rear cockpit, said Don. Chelson labored around the biplane's wing. He stepped up on the wing, and then lifted himself into the seat. As he began to settle down on the seat, he found that he didn't have room sit down.

"That's another problem," said Irvin. "We need to get the pack smaller so that we can fit them inside the biplane cockpit."

"Well what should I do?" asked Chelson.

"Get as low as you can," said Don.

"That is it?" asked Chelson as he crouched on the seat. The large pack lay over the fuselage behind the cockpit.

"Hang on. Once we get up to the 2,000-foot level, get out on the wing. I will turn hard to the side you are standing on and pull up. Jump at that moment. The Jenny will be well out of your way," said Don.

"Sure," said Chelson. "Let's tie this cord that opens the 'chute' on a strut before we forget."

"That's right," said Irvin. "We don't want you to jump without your parachute opening."

When the cord that opened the "chute" was tied down, the Jenny was ready. Moments later. The biplane was taxiing down the grass field.

I stood and watched as the aircraft circled and climbed ever higher. Chelson made his way out of the cockpit while the Jenny began to turn and climb again. Another moment past before I saw Chelson drop off the wing. In another moment, the white "chute" unfolded in the clear blue sky. He floated downward. I knew then that I had to do it myself. I enjoyed the feeling of flying, but floating down must be great.

We retrieved the parachute from the water and stretched it out in the sun to dry. Chelson complained that the water was cold and that he was lucky that there was a tourist nearby to pick him up because our hired boat was too far away. None of that made any difference to me. I was used to cool water. I was going to jump the next day no matter what.

The next day, the weather was as good as it had been the day before. I was excited at the thought of putting on that pack and floating down. I made my way to the landing field, to the spot where I had helped spread the parachute out for drying. Don was there staring at the silk "chute".

"What's the matter with that parachute?" I asked as I stepped close enough to Don to see what it looked like.

"I couldn't figure it out for a time, but it looks like the linen thread Irvin used has shrunk a bit but the silk didn't shrink at all," said Don.

"I guess he will have to use silk thread next time," I said.

"Yeah, I think so," he said. He leaned forward and gave the seams a tug.

"It should be good enough for my jump today," I said.

"Well, I don't know," said Don. "I wish Irvin hadn't gone back home yesterday. I could ask him."

"We won't use it again after my jump," I said.

"I guess that is a good idea. Help me fold this so that we can get ready."

"Sure Don. I would like to jump into the lake before there are too many boats out there."

"Sounds like a good idea," said Don. In a few minutes, the parachute had been packed roughly into

155

the cloth case it was supposed to fit in. I pulled the inner tubes on and buckled the belts. When I pulled the pack on, I was surprised at how heavy it felt.

"Let's go," called Don.

I labored around the wing and stepped up. It was hard to lift myself into the cockpit. I was smaller than Chelson, but I still couldn't sit down. Don stepped up on the wing and looked at me.

"You forgot to tie the cord on the strut," he said. He pulled the cord from the pack. He pulled on it and then tied the end to the strut on the wing.

I was struck by how cold it was to be kneeling in the seat in the back cockpit with only my bathing suit on. I only got colder when it came time to step out onto the wing. As the airplane began to turn and climb, I jumped off the wing. There was no need to worry about hitting the plane; it was gone too fast to worry.

Chelson hadn't told me the most important part of parachuting: once the "chute" opens the yank was incredibly hard. The pain shocked me. The second part I should have paid more attention to what Chelson had said about the cold water. I had no idea how long I had floated in the air before hitting the water, but I wished that it had been longer. Even with the inner tubes around my waist, I still went right under the water. It was so cold out in the middle of the lake that I lost my breath. I was dragged into the boat of a passer-by in short order. I didn't care about the rough way I had been handled. I was just happy to get out of the cold.

We pulled the parachute out of the water and laid it out for drying again. The threads shrank even more than the last time. The "chute" we sent back to the United States was a wrinkled mess.

I was glad I had jumped that day. I had been the first Canadian to use to the packed parachute in Canada. Those jumps at Crystal Beach were just tests, but on July 21st, two American pilots were wearing Irvin's "chutes" when their airplane went out of control. Both bailed out and were saved as their biplane crashed.

20. Winging it Over the Rockies

I remember the summer of 1919. There were many ideas about how airplanes could be used. Some thought air travel should be made available to the public, but only a few believed that would happen.

I pressed my forehead against the pane of glass as I stared down through the window of the airliner. The mountains look like a tiny contour map of the Canadian Rockies. I find it hard to believe that the plane is as high as it is with almost no turbulence.

When I sit in my seat, I notice a woman sitting in the center seat grinning at me. She is probably thinking, 'look at that old man. He is on his way to Vancouver. I bet this is his first time on an airplane'. Well, I guess I must have appeared to be looking at the wonders of the world for a moment. I have to admit that I haven't flown that much in these new jet liners. I feel strange in such a comfortable seat while flying.

Well, to me I'm not flying. To me, flying means being the pilot. I am just sitting here.

I wonder what that woman would say if I told her that I am Ernest C. Hoy, Captain Ernest. She would look at me in an understanding way—an old man looking for someone to talk to. She wouldn't know much about Canadian aviation history. Not too many know that I was the first one to fly over the Canadian Rockies in 1919. That was when I was really flying. Few would have any idea what that was like anyway. It was not like being in this floating bus in the sky. Most biplanes did not have the power to fly high enough to go over the mountains. Pilots wove around the higher peaks because there was no other way. Well, I'm getting ahead of myself here.

I guess my story began when I was a soldier of the 48th Battalion during the First World War in the trenches of France. Like many others, I was wounded in 1917. I didn't like the idea of going back into the mud that was up to my knees or higher. I remember looking up at the biplanes flying over the trenches when I was standing there in the mud. That was what I wanted to do. I wanted to join the Royal Flying Corps. Of course, there were the stories that the army told you about: the Air Corps had a very high casualty rate; you'll regret it; it's cold up there; you're not really fighting because you can't see the white of your enemy's eyes—what rubbish. I wasn't convinced. I was in and through training in no time.

1918 was close to the end of the war, but we didn't know that then. We worked hard to win the war even though we could only fly in clear skies. One day in

September 1918, I went up and came down some time later—in enemy territory. I was a prisoner for two months before the end of the war.

In 1919, I was a member of the British Columbia branch of the Aerial League of Canada. The idea to fly over the Rockies did not come from a few boys just talking. The Vancouver *Daily World*, the *Lethbridge Herald*, the *Calgary Herald*, and the town of Golden, British Columbia sponsored the flight.

The question was who was going to be the pilot? That matter had to be settled in the traditional way; we each put a piece of paper with our name on it into a hat. I didn't think my name would be drawn, but I put it in just for the fun of it. Later, I found myself at the center of the campaign to go over the top, or more likely through the peaks.

The only plane available was the standard Curtiss Jenny. There was nothing fancy about that machine. The Jenny had only one problem: its tank only held 12 gallons of fuel. We fixed that by installing an extra 28-gallon tank on the front seat of the biplane. I didn't worry about having that tank in front of me because I wasn't planning to crash. The exhaust and flying sparks didn't worry me either. In those days, we just flew, hoping for the best. Well, the extra fuel was an improvement anyway.

Now, remember that even though the Jenny was a well-built airplane, it was limited in what it could do. Once you were in the air, if flying conditions were ideal, you could get up to a speed of 75 miles an hour. With the new tank, the plane could fly for about four hours.

I was ready to go on August 4. There were a few items that I had to take along to mark the flight. The first was a package of forty-five letters, specially marked for the day. As if that wasn't enough, I was given a batch of Vancouver's *Daily World*, each addressed to the mayors of the communities that I had to land at for refueling, including Vernon, Cranbrook, Lethbridge, and Calgary.

I remember my first take off on August 4th. The sky was not as clear and bright as I had hoped, but I thought that the weather would improve. The Jenny rumbled down the field then slowly climbed into the air. I was hoping that the aircraft would be able to fly higher as the fuel tanks emptied. If the machine could just climb a little as the plane got lighter that would help.

Unfortunately, the weather got worse. The sky became more and more misty and cloudy. Near the town of Chilliwack, I could see that the clouds were too thick to navigate through the Cheam range of mountains. I didn't want to fly into a cloud that had a rock in it! I turned the Jenny around, and then headed back to Vancouver. I had to wait for a better day to make the flight.

The skies were clear on August 7, 1919. I wasn't taking any chances that day. I was going to get an early start. At 4:13 AM, my Jenny was rumbling down the racetrack at the Minoru Park on Lulu Island. I could see Chilliwack and the Cheam range beyond it at 5:00 in the morning.

A large number of people were at Vernon when I landed at 7:18 AM and later at Grand Forks. Each time

162

I landed, there was a large crowd with many questions. I felt like a barn stormer at a summer fair except there was no time for stunts. At 2:05 PM, I landed in Cranbrook for another refueling. The flight was going well.

For the most part, I was still flying over the lower ranges of mountains. The higher ranges were still in front of me as I taxied down the field at Cranbrook at 3:35 PM on my last leg to Lethbridge. I thought that the Jenny, with her little 90-horse power engine would be able to climb higher than expected if I just tried hard enough. I was wrong! I was never able to get higher than 7,000 feet. I navigated through the Crawford Pass at that height. In many places, the plane was only 150 feet above the rocks and the treetops. The sight of mountain peaks towering over me as the ground appeared to come closer to my wheels made me nervous as I wove through the pass.

As I flew over an out-crop in the rock, I heard a thrust and bang. I was thrown to a higher altitude faster than before. My sudden ascent gave me a feeling of relief. It must have been caused by a thermal. After I had gotten used to the new height, my harness grasped me tight. The air seemed to have pushed out from under the airplane. I had never felt such updrafts and downdrafts in my life. I soon realized that when there was an updraft, there would be a downdraft shortly after. I strained through one sequence of drafts to the next, always trying to keep the aircraft climbing and away from the rock cliffs.

My muscles ached as the huge rocky faces gave way to ever smoother hills and finally to open prairie.

Lethbridge was not much further away. I couldn't wait to land.

A huge crowd had gathered below. It must have been the entire population of Lethbridge. The crowd applauded as I got out of the cockpit, then a tall man in a black suit stepped forward and said, "How do you do?"

"Fine, just fine, now that I am on the ground."

"We would like to welcome you to our town."

"Thank you, sir."

"I am the mayor and…"

"Well, good to meet you," I said as I shook his hand quickly.

"Well, I…"

"I'd hate to hurry, but what time is it?"

"Well it is about half past six."

"Thank you. As soon as the men have the Jenny refueled; I have to move on. There are only a few hours before sunset. I can't fly or land in the dark."

"Feel free to stay in Lethbridge."

"I hope these will be well received," I said as I pulled the package of newspapers from the storage pit at the side of the aircraft.

"They will indeed, thank you."

The mayor, I am sure, had a much grander vision of my stop. Perhaps, he wanted to give a speech, but I didn't have time. I hated to think about landing the Jenny without much more than a prayer. The mayor looked funny standing on the ground watching me bounce down the field. I could almost hear him saying, "You can't just take off."

Flying the rest of the way was going to be easy, but I had to hurry in order to land in Calgary before nightfall. The red-orange sunset on the horizon was beautiful. I could see the lights of the city as I approached. When I got near the landing field, I felt relieved when I saw gasoline flares and hundreds of car lights along the side of the runway. In spite of the poor lighting, or maybe because of it, I touched the plane down perfectly.

"Welcome Mr. Hoy! Welcome!" I heard that before I had even shut the engine off. A delegation of men was approaching me.

"How do you do," said one of them, "I'm the post master."

"Well, then you will want this," I said as I handed him the package of letters.

"Thank you."

"I guess that ends the formalities," I said.

As hard as it was to believe, the reports said that there were 5,000 people in the crowd at Calgary. The newspaper reporters talked with me next.

"How will you get back if the flying is as difficult as it is?"

"Difficult?"

"The turbulences you told us about."

"I'll fly back; after all what's the point in flying one way if the flight can't be repeated?"

"Do you think that flight over the mountains could be carried out on a regular basis, sir?"

"Of course—mind you, every pilot going over for the first time will have a new experience."

"Do you anticipate any difficulties going back?"

165

"No, I can't say I do."

That was it.

The day set for my return was August 11, 1919. At ten minutes to ten on that date, I was lifting off the airfield. I had to circle the aircraft up to a height of 5,000 feet before going west. The flight back seemed much easier. The town of Golden came into view at 12:30 PM. The Selkirk range I had just flown through was much higher than I could fly; the mountain peaks were above me as I went through. Of course, the plane was thrown around by the drafts, but now I knew how to handle the Jenny better when that happened.

With the clear skies, landing wasn't difficult, especially at Golden where the ground altitude was 2,583 feet; I didn't have far to fly down! The people there wanted me to land in the fair grounds, but there was not enough space. I flew on until I found a hay field to land in. After a two-hour stay, I was ready to go. I had to be careful because I had a lot of fuel on board. With the high altitude, there was no chance to correct mistakes.

Because the field was flat, I was confident that I could get the Jenny off the ground. I had to achieve a high speed and height as fast as I could. When the wheels were lifting off the ground everything was fine. If I kept this rate of ascent, I would just miss the top of the cottonwood at the end of the field. I pushed the throttle forward and the engine was roaring as I aimed down the field. The biplane picked up speed for the takeoff. What was THAT! IT'S A COUPLE BOYS RUNNING ACROSS THE FIELD—RIGHT IN FRONT OF THE PROP!

I pulled back hard and pushed the rudder all the way to the right, sliding hard. I wasn't high enough! I jerked one way, then the other. The aircraft came to a stop. The motor was dead. All I heard was a distant voice. I wasn't hurt. I unlatched myself then got out of the cockpit. The flight was over with the wing crushed on the right side and the cover over the motor ripped away. There wasn't even a splinter left where the propeller had been.

"Are you all right?" asked the mayor as he rushed to the side of the aircraft.

"Sure. What time does the train go through for Vancouver?"

"Train?"

"Yeah, I need to get this pack of letters into the city as quickly as possible. I will be back to get the wreck later in the week."

"Well..."

I don't remember what happened to the Jenny. I can't remember going back for it either. The flight was over. The Curtiss Jennies were so cheap to buy that there was no reason to rescue a wrecked one. A museum might want it today, but then, we didn't think we were involved in a monumental first flight. We were just interested in seeing what could be done with the aircraft that was all.

21. Bank Robbery Scoop by Airplane

I was a reporter with the *Winnipeg Free Press* in the 1920s. I'm Cecil Lamont. One of the most interesting stories I remember from my years at the *Free Press* happened in the fall of 1920. I got up early that day not expecting anything different. That was about to change as I stepped into the editorial offices.

No one was sitting at the desks typing yet. As a matter of fact, I was the only one in the newsroom. I turned around, looked at the empty desks and thought that everyone else must be bored with their work too. My gaze stopped at the editor's office. The lights were on. The editor was sitting at his desk and talking on the telephone. I figured it would not be long before he would ask me to make the coffee. I went to the corner of the office where the coffee machine was sitting.

"Hey!" came a call from the editor's office. "Who is that? Cecil is that you?"

"Yeah, I am about to make some coffee."

169

"Don't worry about that. Get in here right now!"

I didn't say a word as I rushed into his office.

"I was on the phone," continued the editor. "It is a big story. I need someone now. You're going to be covering it. You're going to have to move fast."

"Sure, what is it?" I said, feeling relieved that I would be doing something different today.

"We got a message this morning that there was a major bank robbery in a village just south of here. Winkler is its name. I think it was a big robbery that was planned by a large, organized group."

"Why large and organized?" I asked.

"We just started to get the story over the phone when the line went dead. Not only are they organized enough to rob the town's bank early in the morning when no one would expect it, they had enough people to have cut the telephone lines."

"Should I write up what we know, then drive down there?" I asked.

"No, you have time to do a better story than that."

"It is going to take far too long to drive down there to talk to people, then issue the story even if I stop at a town where the phones are working to phone the story in."

"I was thinking about that this morning. I have a new idea of how we can get this story finished on time to have it in the evening paper."

"How?" I asked.

"I have been watching that new flying company on the outskirts of the city. I figure we should hire one of those planes to get down there fast; that is if you aren't afraid of flying."

"I really wanted to try flying out. I like that idea," I said.

"Good. You get out to that airport while I make the necessary arrangements," said the editor.

"Sure I'm on my way," I said.

"Hey, Cecil! What's the name of that flying company?" called the editor.

"Oh, I think it is the Canadian Aircraft Company," I said as I stepped out of the office. I was on my way in a few moments. I hoped that the people who were running that flying company would be ready to go when I arrived.

I raced to the aerodrome. I was relieved to see that the biplane's motor was already running. When I jumped out of the car, one of the pilots confronted me.

"Are you Cecil Lamont?" yelled the man over the loud roar of the motor.

"Yes!" I called back.

"Here, put these on and I'll show you where to sit," the pilot handed me a set of goggles. He pulled me toward the airplane in a hurry.

"You are sitting in the front seat of the back cockpit!" yelled the man. "Frank is our mechanic. He'll be sitting right behind you!"

"Okay, that sounds fine!"

In a moment, I was sitting down. I couldn't see the front. The biplane looked more like a farm tractor than a flying machine. In a moment, we were rushing down the field. The back end of the aircraft came up, then we lifted off the ground. We turned south. Without gaining much altitude, the biplane raced to the village that was seventy-four miles away. It was in the middle of the harvest season. As we flew, we could see dust clouds where crews were already hard at work on their threshing machines.

I was not even accustomed to flying yet when we arrived at the outskirts of Winkler. The flight took only forty-two minutes. I jumped out of the airplane and hurried into town. The pilot was far behind. I just had a rough idea of where the Union Bank was, but it took only a few minutes to get there. I rushed into the front door of the bank and stared at the debris that was lying around. There was now a hole in the wall where the vault used to be. Everything was a mess of bricks and mortar. The air was still stinging with the smell of sulfur and smoke.

I had only looked around for a moment when I heard a small voice behind me.

"Who are you?" he asked.

"I'm Cecil Lamont from the *Winnipeg Free Press*."

"You sure got here fast," he said.

"I had a ride on a airplane. How much was taken?"

"I'm the teller here. By my last count, there was something like $19,000 in cash and bills. It is all gone now."

"When did you realize there had been a robbery?"

"Before it happened," said the little man with a quiver in his voice.

"Oh?"

"I have my quarters in the back, you know. I was sleeping like everyone else when they broke the door in. I barely had a chance to roll over in bed when a couple of these masked guys put ropes on me. They tied my hands and feet." He stopped and looked around in silence for a moment.

"Then what happened?"

"They were talking about blowing the safe. They wanted the robbery to go fast after the blast went off because the noise would wake up the whole town. I told them that I had been overseas during the First World War and that I had been severely shell shocked. I told them that they should move me away before they blasted the safe."

"What did they say to that?" I asked.

"The leader said he had been in the war too. He figured he could help me out. Some of the guys dragged me to the house nearby and put blankets over me to lesson the sound of the blast."

"Do you know how they basted the safe?"

"They dynamited the vault to get to the inner safe. After they had that done, they used a sledgehammer to knock off the combination knob. Then they poured liquid nitroglycerine into the hole and set it off."

"The town's people had to have been awakened by the first blast. Where were they?"

"Oh, they came out all right, but ask any of them, and they will tell you that the whole village was patrolled by bandits. They all had shot guns."

"No one acted to stop them?"

"Yes, there was a blacksmith. He hurried out to sound the fire alarm because he thought his fire had caused the explosion, but he was shot at. He crawled back to his house. I saw him get help later. No one dared to try to stop them after that. Before we knew it, the cars were gone. We drove out to phone Winnipeg."

173

I was taking notes on everything the teller was saying. I was happy that the mechanic was an enthusiastic photographer because he was moving around the ruins of the bank taking photographs as I prepared my story. We walked back to the biplane, talking to excited villagers as we went. Since the teller told me all the details, few changes had to be made. I sat down on the wing of the biplane to check the story one last time. The villagers were still talking to the pilot and the mechanic about the robbery. They didn't seem to notice the biplane. That was strange because flying was still a novelty to most of these people.

The editor was glad to see that the story was finished when I arrived at the office. We were the only newspaper to have the story of the biggest bank robbery in Canada that evening. It was clear to me that the biplane would be used for more stories like this more often in the future.

22. Business in the Bush

We call them bush pilots. Most Canadians know what that means without any explanation; that is, they know what bush is and what a pilot is. To me a bush pilot is someone who is a bit wild and enjoys flying by instinct into unknown places. Of course, a bush pilot's most important task is to keep returning for another flight somewhere. Remember that even when he goes on daring flights, a bush pilot still needs some common sense. He has to know what he can get away with. That comes from experience and from talking to other pilots who flew before. The stories about those first pilots who went out into the bush are interesting because even though they had common sense and a desire for adventure, they had never flown over the wilderness.

Now, I was involved in one of those first commercial flights. I can't say that it was number one because who knows if someone else had been up north or over the bush before us. The independence of the

175

early pilots makes it hard to say exactly who was the first to fly deep into the bush and back as part of a commercial enterprise.

I must add that I wasn't the pilot on October 15, 1920 when we flew to The Pas in Manitoba. I am Frank Ellis, the flight engineer. Hector Dougall was the pilot.

In the summer of 1920, the Canadian Aircraft Company employed me. It was a general company for hire for whatever kind of flying was needed. We transported people here and there, barnstormed, and that was about it. Like many other small aviation companies that were started after the First World War, we bought old Avro biplanes with 110 horse power *Le Rohne* rotary engines from the British government. We didn't bother repainting the plane like many other small companies had done, but we did covert it from a two seater to a three seater. We used the extra seat for passengers and for cargo.

Even though we were willing to fly many places, we were surprised when Frank J. Stanley, a fur trader, walked into our offices in Winnipeg in October 1920 and asked if we would fly him home to The Pas. The Pas was about two hundred miles over some of the roughest regions of Manitoba's bush, but we agreed to fly him there anyway.

"Hector, what do you think about that job?" I asked my partner as Stanley disappeared out the door.

"Well, we have to take whatever work comes our way."

"We'll be taking a big chance. There is nothing but muskeg, trees, and no where to land with wheels."

"You mean land comfortably."

"I mean land at all."

"Well, look at it this way, we have wanted to go on a good fishing trip—this may be our chance to do it for free."

"You mean at the cost of one airplane and…"

"Don't worry about that."

"What about fuel? We will have to stop for fuel. We'll need a supply in The Pas when we got there. That is if we want to make it back."

"A community as large as The Pas will have fuel."

"What if there is no fuel there?"

"Well, we wanted a fishing trip."

"That sounds like fun in the snow."

"Don't worry. We have to get ready for the flight."

"I'll pack for the fishing trip."

"That sounds like a good idea, Frank."

We were ready to take off on October 15, 1920 at 11:00 in the morning. As the flight engineer, I was standing in the front of the biplane ready to give it a flip to start. Frank Stanley was in the seat waiting as I yelled to Dougall. I gave the motor one more flip and it roared. I walked around the biplane and got into my seat. We all buckled up our harnesses as the ground man pulled away the chocks allowing us to move.

As we lifted off from the ground, we saw only clear warm skies. If the weather remained clear and calm, then we would soon be landing at The Pas. After a few minutes, we could see smoke rising from the chimneys of Portage la Prairie. Fifteen minutes later, we were focused on getting to Gladstone. We could see the huge stretch of Lake Manitoba to the north—water stretched to the vanishing point.

At Gladstone, we had a problem—the engine was skipping and coughing. We had to land and find out what the trouble was. Hector saw a smooth field at the edge of the town and came in for a landing. I found a bad spark plug, fixed it, and then we were ready to take off.

Soon, we were high in the sky heading for the community of Dauphin, only about ninety air miles away. We circled higher to fly around the eastern side of Riding Mountain. An hour and twenty minutes later, we were landing in another ploughed field at Dauphin. After flying during the summer, we agreed that it was better to land near a possible fuel source even if we had to land in a rough field. Walking a few miles wasn't a good idea.

When the aircraft came to a stop, the scene was just like a summer fair. Everyone in town was waiting for us. Cars pulled up around the plane. We had no trouble finding a ride. In a few minutes, we were at a garage to get some gasoline. We had to hurry to take off before dark.

Soon, we had taken off towards Duck River. We climbed high, circled Duck Mountain to the east, and then Hector turned the biplane west. We were lucky when we landed at Swan River at half past six in the evening just as the light faded. We jumped down from the airplane and anchored it in place. The Inn in town was about a mile away. The hike felt like fifty miles to me.

* * *

We watched out the door as the rain began to fall again. The morning was fading away.

"Do you think that we will make it today?" ask Frank Stanley.

"All we need is a break in the rain long enough to take off, then we'll make it," said Hector.

"Well, it doesn't look good," said Stanley.

"You know what they always say," I said.

"What?"

"The sun is always shining above the clouds," I said. Hector grinned, but Stanley continued to look grim and tired.

"It really is cold today, too," Stanley muttered.

I was getting a bit annoyed. It wasn't just one of those days when it rains continuously. It stopped raining, then just as we were ready to go it would start falling again. All we could do was sit down and have another coffee. I must say that I had too many coffees; I was beginning to feel terrible. Just when I thought all chances of taking off had passed, Hector announced:

"This is it for today—we take off now or we will be stuck here for another day." Picking up our bags with a sense of urgency, we rushed out the door. It seemed like only a few minutes, Hector and Stanley were in the cockpit. We were shouting the commands to each other as fast as we could. The engine was primed with fuel, the ignition was thrown on and in a moment the engine started. After I hopped in, we were off. That was at 2:30 AM—not much time before the sunset. We headed straight for The Pas. We hoped to

179

get there and back before nightfall so that we could make it to Winnipeg the next day.

Unfortunately, the clouds closed in again. In those days, the idea that we could fly above the clouds was a joke. We couldn't navigate without landmarks. There wouldn't be an easy flight straight to The Pas. Our contingency plan was to fly to the village of Hudson Bay Junction in Saskatchewan. We could land there and stay over night if we needed to. If the weather improved, we could always head back to The Pas without landing. It would be just another hop like we were used to doing in the summer barnstorming season.

The flight was rough. We were wet from the rain. As we flew the one hundred and nine miles over the Porcupine Mountains, there was a lot of turbulence. The rain ended when it began to snow heavily. Blind, we pushed on. That is not to say that we had run out of luck; we had been very lucky to stay on our course. We had to fly in different directions to avoid the worst of the snow squalls. We flew really low, just above the treetops so that we could keep some sense of direction and maintain visual contact with the ground.

I felt a sense of relief when I saw the small buildings and the fine lines of smoke rising from the chimneys in the village of Hudson Bay Junction. We flew over the community and began to circle. I knew what Hector was looking for: a good field to land on. But I saw what he did; there didn't seem to be a clearing in the bush big enough for us to land.

I felt uneasy. I thought that this would be one of the problems if we came this far into the bush. We flew in wider and wider circles. There was no farmland, just bush and muskeg in all directions.

We didn't have much fuel left. If we tried to fly on to The Pas, we would never make it flying against heavy head winds. Yet, the wind was about to become our ally. We swung around to face right into it, and then we came down, approaching an area of muskeg. The wind slowed our ground speed to about 30 miles per hour, slower and much safer then usual.

When we touched the ground, our wheels just kept on going down until the muck and swamp grass was up to our axles. We stopped with a powerful jerk. The full strain of the landing was on the hardwood undercarriage. The tail of the biplane jumped up as the nose started to go down. We were lucky that the motion stopped before the nose was down far enough to shatter the propeller. We didn't realize it at that moment, but the plane was miraculously saved from any damage.

The entire population of the small village was already by the aircraft as we pulled ourselves out of the machine. They got a free barnstorming show, which they appreciated. No one there had ever seen an airplane before. There were questions to answer as we worked to get the machine out of the mud. With that much excitement, it didn't take any effort at all to get enough help to move the biplane out of the muck.

Another group of men immediately set to work clearing a stretch of bush for our take off. Even though we had only two hours of daylight, we were able to get part of the runway cleared and push the biplane to it by dusk. Were invited to stay as guests for the night. We were kept up late into the night talking about what we had done that summer.

When we woke up the next morning, most of the locals were already at work clearing the runway. By early afternoon, there was a rough area that would work for a take-off even though it was very short.

Hector thanked the man in charge. "There is one more thing we need before we can be on our way."

"Just name it," said the husky man.

"We need some fuel."

"Fuel?"

"You know, gas for the engine to fly out of here."

"Like gas for cars?"

"The same."

"We don't have roads. We don't have any gas because we don't need it here."

"What?" said Hector, bewildered.

"Not a drop. Are you sure you don't have enough in that machine to take off? The weather is good."

"No, not at all. We landed here because we need more fuel."

"I can't say I have anything I can give you."

"What is it you say?" said a small Chinese man who as among the crowd.

"We need gasoline."

"Ah, yes. Gas we have."

"Are you sure?" asked Hector.

"I don't know," said the husky man. "His English isn't that good. He runs the laundry and the café."

"I understand," protested the man.

"Well, how do you have any gas?"

"I show you," said the man as he turned and ran back to the small group of buildings.

"I don't know Hector," said the other again.

"Well, we can follow him to see if he does have something we can use."

A few moments later the small man came out of the café carrying two four-gallon cans very carefully. We could see that he was walking with the greatest of care. Soon, he was by us with the two cans. I stepped forward, kneeled down and smelled the liquid.

"Yeah, this is real. It actually smells like a very high grade gasoline at that."

"Great!" yelled Hector as he grabbed the man and hugged him. He got hold of himself and shook hands with the small man. "Why do you have this fuel here?"

"I need it for lamps and heater. It is very good, yes?"

"Yes, thank you. How much will that cost?"

"For you, nothing."

We couldn't believe our luck. That is not to say that we thought we were all lucky. We thought that we were being blessed with two opposites. If we weren't getting very bad luck, we were getting very good luck. It was half past three when we climbed aboard the biplane again. Of course, we didn't have enough room to make a normal take off. We had to recruit the men in the village for one more task.

Because we needed as much power as we could get before we tried to leave the ground, we tied a rope to the back of the airplane. The men had to hold the machine back until the engine was at full throttle, then we would give them the sign to let go.

The engine roared, Hector gave the signal and the biplane lurched forward, speeding up fast. The plane was at the end of the short runway in no time. Hector pulled back on the stick. I could hear our under carriage sweep through the brush just beyond the clearing. In front of us were huge trees. Hector pulled hard on the stick to turn, sweeping clear by only a few inches. We circled the village a few times to gain altitude and to wave back to the village one last time.

We took an eastward direction at 3,000 feet. The sky was clear. All you could see as we flew on was the unbroken distance of lakes, water, trees and swampy muskeg. I had brought a camera along. I decided the scene would make a good photograph. I struggled for a moment to get it out, looked through the viewfinder and wished that I could get a wide angle.

The strong tail wind reassured me. The eighty-seven miles that we had to fly slipped by quickly. The Pas was in sight in about forty minutes. This time there would not be any difficulty landing because there were cultivated fields. We chose to land behind the Lumber Company. As we came in to land, we could see that the field that appeared to be so smooth was covered with stumps. Lucky for us we bounced to a stop without hitting one.

The town's people were waiting for us when we landed. They had received a telegraph message. Mayor Stitt and all the town counselors were on hand, not to congratulate Hector for the flight, but to congratulate Frank Stanley for being the first passenger to fly into the north. They even had a banquet for him the next day.

We did get recognition in the local newspaper, *The Pas Weekly Herald.* The newspaper reported that, "The first airplane to invade the solitude of the hinterland arrived in The Pas from Winnipeg on Sunday afternoon at 4:30, with Pilot Dougall, Air Mechanic Ellis and Frank Stanley passenger. The machine left the capital city at 11 AM on Friday after returning from Winkler in search of the robbers who blew the Union Bank safe. Stops were made at Gladstone, Dauphin, Swan River and H.B. Junction for gasoline. Forty-two minutes was the flying time from the Junction to The Pas..."

We remained in The Pas for a week giving locals rides as if it was a summer fair. We had our fishing trip. The flying season of 1920 was more or less over for us.

23. Racing to the Klondike and Beyond

The most memorable flight I ever had occurred in the summer of 1920. During that summer, I was a pilot for the U.S. Army Service. Our task was to survey the Northwest Staging Route. It was to be an important route for flying north as far as Alaska. Later, it was important in the Second World War as an air route to Russia. The first time the route was surveyed was in that summer.

When we set out from New York for Canada, we were not thinking about going to the Arctic Circle to survey a route for the future generations. We were thinking about our goal. It was to get to Dawson City in the Yukon in time for the annual summer Klondike fair. There was a certain excitement in flying north to the trails that men and women walked in 1898 to get to the gold fields of the Yukon. We were expecting to have a much better trip than they had back then. We

187

First Flights

were in for a big surprise. We had no idea how long it would take or how hard it would be. That was certainly an adventure. If we had a full understanding of how bad the cold and snow could be, we would have all been much more hesitant.

We set out with eight airmen and four biplanes. These were not the small aircraft that people were used to. These were four huge De Havilland 4Bs. Each had an engine with twelve cylinders and four hundred-horse power. The biplanes each carried twelve gallons of oil and had fuel tanks that held one hundred and twenty gallons. All of them had the U.S. Army Service insignia, a wolf's head, on the side.

The aircraft were number from one to four. Our leader was Captain St. Claire Streett who was in machine No. 1 with Edmund Henriques. In the second aircraft was Clifford Nutt and myself, Erik Nelson. I was an engineering officer. Crumrine and Long manned the next machines. Ross Kirkpatrick and Joe English were in No. 4. We all wore heavy cotton flying suites that looked more like overalls that car mechanics wear. As usual for those days, we had heavy leather helmets and goggles.

After we took off from New York on July 15, 1920, we flew through the mid-western States to Portal, North Dakota. Then on July 25, we crossed the border and flew to Saskatoon. It felt less like a military operation as we flew across the warm summer sky of the Canadian prairies. We were relaxed and full of anticipation as we approached the landing field built by Stan McClelland in Saskatoon. We would not be setting up tents when we arrived there because we had rooms at the local hotel, the King George. When we got out of our aircraft, there was already a porter from the hotel waiting. We didn't have much luggage to give the man, but I'm sure he wasn't too upset about that. He looked excited as he walked around the biplanes, staring at every detail.

"How far did you fly today?" the porter asked.

"We flew for about four and half hours from Portal, North Dakota."

"What were the prairies like to fly over?"

"The best part of the trip. There weren't too many turbulent areas. The crops were like a checkerboard. It is so flat that when we were coming into Saskatoon, we could see it from forty miles away."

It was not long before we were at the hotel. There was a small crowd clapping. Some people asked for our autographs. One girl even asked the porter for his. The manager shook Captain Streett's hand and invited him into the hotel.

When Streett had sat down at the special table set for us in the café the door opened, a boy from the telegraph office came in.

"Is there a Captain Streett here?" he asked. We all stared at the captain for a moment.

"Yes, over here," said the hotel manager. The boy walked over and handed the captain the piece of paper. Captain Streett stared a moment at the note. We did not want to ask any questions, but we all wanted to know what it said.

"It's from the Canadian government..." he voice faded. His statement did not assure us. "It's from the

189

Canadian Air Board at Ottawa," he continued. He remained stern and unmoved.

"Sir, is it good news?" asked the manger.

"Oh, quite good. It congratulates us on our progress and gives best wishes for the rest of the trip."

The night went as planned. There was a dinner, then a small stage show for the airmen and a social.

After the evening's events I made my way up to my room. I had a feeling that the easy flying would not continue all the way to the Arctic Circle. I just wanted to get to bed and rest as much as I could before flying on the next day. The bed was so comfortable that I was asleep in no time. We would have an early start tomorrow. We had to get up and check the machines over, then head to Edmonton. Even if the flight were easy, it would be a long day.

There were no problems with the airplanes and the check was completed quickly. Just as fast we were in the air.

As we set out west to Edmonton, we did not expect too much excitement. There were no formal arrangements for airfields. As far as I knew, there were no accommodations set up for us. We flew down the Battle river valley. We were getting close to the city. On the horizon, we could see a number of biplanes approaching us. They came in close and waved. That was a nice gesture, I thought. Soon, we saw a clearing near the city. Captain Streett headed down. Our four airplanes circled and landed, but the two Curtiss Jennies that had followed us circled another time. I expected them to wave their wings one more time and then fly on, but they landed. One of the pilots jumped out and ran over to where we stood.

"Captain Streett!" he called as he walked close. Streett nodded his head and the man stepped in front of him. "Captain 'Wop' May," he said as he put his hand out to shake.

"How do you do?" responded Streett.

"Fine, until now, sir," he said.

"Oh, really?"

"You were supposed to follow us to the another field to land," said May.

"Oh? I didn't know that there was supposed to be an official landing field," Streett commented.

"There is nothing official about it," said May.

"Oh? Well then what is this all about?"

"A local welcome. There are a lot of people waiting to see these planes and show you a good time."

"That is fine," said Streett, smiling.

In a moment, there were three more men standing with May, who had run ahead of the party.

"These two men are here to be as official as anyone can be," said May as he stepped aside and let two men step forward.

"Hello, I'm Acting Mayor James East and this is Alderman Charles Hepburn," said the man.

"How do you do," said Streett nearly laughing now.

"Well, could I have you take off again and land at the exhibition grounds as we had hoped you would?"

"Certainly," said Streett.

In a few moments, we were all taking off from the field. We would be making a grand entrance. First, the

191

small Curtiss biplane landed in the wide stretch of grass. Then we landed. A crowd gathered around us as if it were a touring group of barnstormers scheduled to give a flying exhibition later that afternoon. The grass was warm. Everyone was in high spirits. This was going to be a good couple of days to relax and get ready for the big push north.

A few days had passed by July 31st. We were up early and preparing for the flight to Jasper. The first major obstacle we had to face was the Rocky Mountains. I didn't think too much about flying through the mountains until I was told that we had to fly over a number of mountains regions that had not been mapped yet. We didn't even know how high some of the mountains were.

That was what this trip was about though. We had to get out there and see whether the flight north was possible and practical. Edmonton was the last point of real comfort before we had to fly over and face the harsh reality of the wilderness.

The day was dark and cloudy as though we had to be warned about what was ahead. We had to take off and go as soon as we were ready. The cool moist air blew against our faces as we speeded along the field. I hoped we could make it to Jasper in one easy flight. After only a short time in the air, it began to rain. We kept going. A little rain was not going to stop us. But, it didn't quit. It increased in its intensity until we were beating against a downpour. The lead biplane began to circle and we followed. We were on our way back to Edmonton. This was the first time that we had to turn back since we left New York.

It made me doubt that the rest of the expedition would be easy. It would be the first time that anyone had flown through the mountains where we planned to fly and then to the Bering Sea. I wanted to be a part of that no matter what.

The sun rose hot the next day. We were off. We pushed west and north. Far below, we saw that the forest was on fire and turned northward to the Athabaska. We flew low over the small town of Pocahontas, then we continued on toward Jasper Lake and Bride's Lake. We were to fly to the point where the Athebaska and the Snaring rivers meet each other. A landing field was supposed to be made there. To everyone's relief, the field was clearly marked. We had no difficulty landing. The superintendent of the National Park, Colonel Maynard Rogers was waiting to greet us.

There was no time at this stop to relax as we had arrived late in the day. We only wanted to get some rest before we had to take off the next day.

The next stop was Prince George. There were a lot of high ranges of mountains between that destination and Jasper. We made that leg of our trip without too much trouble. The mountains were easier to fly than we expected.

But there was some trouble as soon as we got into the air. Captain Streett's machine began to smoke, and then flames burst from his aircraft. Looking at the machine in flight, I realized immediately that an oil line must have broke. He signaled that we were to fly on while he returned for repairs. We weren't supposed to brake up the formation like this, but we had agreed that as long as we were in the south, that is, as long as we were still in the provinces, we would change our formation if we had to. As soon as we got into the Northwest Territories, we would stay together. I wasn't too worried because an oil line could be fixed easily. I expected him to catch up to us in Prince George.

The next problem happened to Crumrine in the third machine when his tire blew out. Added to the blown tire, the propeller was nicked when he landed. The funniest part was when his passenger, Sergeant Long, saw that the machine was going too fast and that the biplane would hit the bushes. He climbed out of his cockpit and slid along the fuselage toward the back, trying to slow it down. That didn't work at all. Before too long, the biplane landed in the bushes and went up on its nose. Old Long was catapulted into the dense bush right over the top of the plane. Long was lucky he was wearing such a thick flight suit. All the dense trees broke his fall. After he landed for the second time, he was all right.

I was right about Streett's biplane. The oil line was quickly repaired. He was up in the air by 1 PM, flew all the way to Prince George, and arrived just as the day was getting dark. Before he arrived, we set up flares to guide him down. There was one complication; a rainstorm that just got worse as the evening went on. By the time Streett was bringing his plane down, the storm was at full strength. Captain Streett made it to a landing, but the lower wing was badly damaged. We all knew that it was damaged; yet no one wanted to look at it. We just wanted to go indoors where it was dry and warm.

It was obvious that we would not be able to go on. Everyone had to stay in Prince George and wait for the repairs to the wing to be complete. There were no aircraft mechanics in Prince George. We hired cabinet builders to do the work. Of course, I had to stay behind to help with the repairs, but Captain Streett and my pilot, Nutt, went by train to Hazelton.

I thought that arrangements had been made for most of our landing sites, but that was not the case. When they got back, they said that the place they had agreed to land at Hazelton turned out to be a field of oats at full length. They corrected the situation by having the farmer cut a wide swath through it. I wasn't sure if they had an agreement to land there before or even if the field was a crop of oats. They could be teasing me; I didn't know. I was satisfied to know that there was a place to land. I would not know if the story was true until we got there.

The day came to take off for the trip north on August 13th. We were in the air by nine in the morning. We arrived in Hazelton at 12:15 PM. As we approached to land, I could see clearly that we were landing in the middle of a field of grain. There was a crowd of people watching as we came down.

Quite a number of people were moving around the planes as we got out. I noticed that Streett was in a small crowd. I walked over to hear what was being said. The small crowd was the group of men who had helped build the landing field.

"It sure looks like the ground was flat enough," said one of the men.

"It was, thank you for the help," said Streett.

195

"We've never seen such machines," said another man.

"I guess there haven't been too many biplanes up here," said Streett.

Streett and Nutt rolled out the existing maps for the northern areas we were flying through. They looked like a trapper's scrawl. There was no information we could use. There were only rough estimations of where the creeks and rivers flowed. There was no mention of the mountains we would be flying over. The solution was to fly as high as we could and to never fly in the skies without clear visibility. Of course, everyone knew that those rules would have to be broken if we wanted to complete our mission.

The situation didn't improve once we had taken off that same day. The sky was full of clouds that became so heavy that we could not see the ground for two hours. After we could see the ground, we figured out that the Nass River was flowing below. After that, we saw the Stewart Arm and the Behm Canal, then Wrangell Island. Finally, we saw Wrangell itself. We landed on Serieff Island. I was surprised to see residents of the island were keeping a smoke smudge going for us. By this time, I was sure that we were flying by the seat of our pants and there had been no planned fields this far north.

I quickly realized that I shouldn't relax too much. The landing was rough and wet. We were sprayed with freezing salt water. The field we had landed on was a meadow of salt marsh grass. The water was a foot deep in places.

I jumped out of the biplane and walked to the group of locals that were greeting Nutt and Streett.

"Is this a bad day?" asked Nutt.

"What do you mean?" asked one of the locals.

The rough field and all that water."

Not at all," he said. "This is good dry day."

"What do you mean?"

"Well, I would say that this is a good time to land and a good day, because this is a salt flat that is covered with about twenty feet of water at tide."

"I suppose we have had a little luck then," said Nutt.

Well, we didn't have it that lucky; Captain Streett had nicked his propeller on the landing. We had a few days stop over. Three of the aircraft were ready to go.

Our next destination was White Horse, over the Stikine River, the Taku Glacier, Juneau, and Skagway. We went right over the White Pass, one of the biggest obstacles for those who were searching for gold in the Klondike gold rush.

When we arrived in White Horse, we were relieved. Our minds turned to the goal we had during the carefree days of flying over the prairies. We wanted to hurry to the celebrations at Dawson City on August 17th. It looked good to us. It was the sixteenth and Dawson City was just one day away. We would be up early tomorrow and be ready to go. However, we had to wait for Streett to arrive with his repaired propeller. We decided that machine No. 3 would wait for No. 1. My airplane, No. 2, and No. 4 were free to fly to Dawson.

I was excited when we took to the air on August 17th. I knew it would not be long before we would be landing in that city of legends, Dawson. It was in the early evening when we made our final approach on Faulkner's Field, just west of Dawson. There was an official welcoming group led by George MacKenzie.

It was not long before I was walking down the boardwalks of the city that was the center of the world only twenty years before. Everyone seemed to want to be here. It was exciting. It was an anniversary party to celebrate the discovery of gold. The dance halls were brightly lit. We had a good time. All my apprehension left me. We would make it to the Bering Sea and back again.

It was great to be there. Everyone knew that our arrival indicated that change was coming to the north. Now that we proved that flight to the north was possible, it would not be long before air travel replaces the steam wheeler on the slow difficult trip north. The north would become less isolated.

The next day, Streett and Long arrived. Streett came into the landing field and told us that they had been delayed because Long's plane had blown a tire. Streett had taken off from White Horse, circled to watch Long take off, and saw that the aircraft curved to one side. He had a second blow out and would take some time to catch up. He had just told us that when we heard the drone of Long's plane. Streett couldn't believe it. Long had filled the tire with fabric and wrapped rope around it. That was done fast and here they were.

On the next day, we took off for the flight to Fairbanks, Alaska. This stop was a relief because the repairs we had been doing to that point had been makeshift. All the spare parts we needed to fix the biplanes properly were waiting at Fairbanks. Even though we arrived late in the afternoon, we set to work replacing parts. We were ready to continue on August 23rd. We were almost all the way to our final destination of Nome.

Without any delays, we were off. It was 5:30 PM when all four machines came to a stop on the old parade grounds at Fort Davis. We got out of our airplanes and walked to the shore of the Bering Sea. After forty days, we had made it. The north looked as it must have for thousands of years. Our trip would not change the north, but it would change the lives of those who lived there. For those people, the north would never be the same again. At least that is how we felt.

We remained on the north shore for three days. We had only completed just half our mission, but it felt like the climax had come and gone. Now, we had to get back to New York. We arrived in Fairbanks the afternoon of August 31st. The planes were carefully inspected and we were ready to fly again on September 3rd. We arrived in Dawson and prepared for the next leg of our trip to White Horse. We would have to hurry the next day because of the early fall storm that was forming. The storms were hitting our tails on the fourth as we landed at White Horse. On the morning of September 5th, the weather looked bad, but we took off hoping to reach Telegraph Creek, B.C. We had not flown long before the severe winds and snow forced us to return to White Horse.

We telegraphed from the Yukon to Telegraph Creek and asked that they send word the first moment that the weather cleared. The message arrived on September 8th. We wasted no time taking to the air. This time we got only halfway before we had to return due to weather. Only three biplanes landed in White Horse. As it turned out, Kirkpatrick had been separated from us and landed at Wrangell. I was never too sure if it was because of good navigation or because he had some friends there, but he made a safe landing.

The next day, we were off again. This time we came in close to Telegraph Creek and landed in a hay field of Diamond C Ranch, twelve miles away from the community. During the landing, the landing gear on Crumrine's machine was severely damaged. We stayed there while Nutt and Streett flew to Wrangell where spare parts were to arrive. They came back on September 18th with the parts to make the repairs. We tried to fly to Hazelton on the 17th and 19th, but were stopped by poor weather. We weren't able to make the trip to Hazelton until September 29th. With determination, we forced our machines through the snow and wind from Hazelton to Edmonton on October 8th. We took off again on October 10th and arrived in Fargo, North Dakota on the 11th. From there, we had clear flying through to New York. We came in for a perfect landing on October 20th at the Mitchell Field, Long Island, New York at 1:37 PM.

We had flown 9,000 air miles in 112 flying hours. With that ended the longest, hardest and most memorable flight of my life. It was the first big northern flight and I was there. The most important part for me wasn't that point when we were looking over the Bering Sea, but the point when we landed at that field outside of Dawson City. I remember thinking about all the stories I had been told about the gold rush. The biggest problem had been getting there. The men that dug in the gold fields had to push through the White Pass. Many never made it. I could see why. Then, I thought how much easier it had been for me in the back cockpit of a biplane. Had any of those men or women who struggled over the White Pass in 1898 looked up and thought of how great it would be to be a bird and fly over?

202

24. The Canadian Air Force Get Their Man

All I really wanted to do was fly, but no matter how hard I tried I couldn't get into the air very long. During the First World War, I had dreamed of being in uniform and flying in the Royal Flying Corps for Canada. I had the right look. I was fit; thin with wide shoulders and light build. I was sure I looked just like any wartime fighter pilot. The problem was that I was too young to join the Flying Corps during the war. There was no Canadian Air Force right after the war. I used every opportunity I could to get off the farm and drive to my neighbor, Barns, who had his own old Curtiss biplane. By the summer of 1920, Barns had let me taxi that plane down the field, but that was all. I wasn't satisfied. I let everyone know that as soon as I could, I would be on my way to a flying school somewhere. I had no idea where I would go, but it didn't matter. I was sure that every city would have a flying school.

I didn't find a flying school right away. Instead, I found the North West Flight Company in Winnipeg. They were happy to have me around as a laborer who was willing to fly and to work at loading and unloading cargo. I would load up a biplane, jump into the back cockpit of the aircraft and take off. The pilot, Alex, gave me a few tips on flying.

"Okay, Fred, what I think you should do is hold on to the stick and feel what I'm doing," he said.

"That sounds fine to me," I replied. I couldn't believe my good fortune.

"We'll have you fly all the time soon. It is easy," said Alex as we climbed into the cockpit.

Even though I had been on two other flights, it seemed all new to me now. I was learning to fly. I noticed the smallest movements of the stick as we taxied down the runway. There was a slight nudge of the stick forward to lift the tail. We sped up, then the stick pulled back and the wheels lifted off the ground. I felt light and free. Soon, we were in the clouds. I imagined that I was alone and free to fly wherever I wanted to. I couldn't wait to fly on my own. Bit by bit, I was allowed to fly more. After four months, I was taking off and landing the airplane for the company.

In September, a stranger arrived at the offices of the North West Flight Company. He asked me to take off with the airplane and fly a figure eight. After I landed, I was told that the man was an officer of the government of Canada and that I had just passed my pilot's license examination.

My work at the company did not change after I had my license. The biggest problem I had was that the company had only two planes. When Alex crashed his biplane in October, I was out of a job.

"Well Fred, I guess you're on your own. You're a pilot now. I figure you could find an airplane for nearly nothing. There are still a lot around from the war," said Alex.

"Thanks for helping me get my pilot's license, but I really don't think I will set up a company. I'll get another job somewhere else." I knew very well that everyone who could fly was setting up flying companies. There were more companies out there than people who wanted to fly with them.

Since I still liked the idea of flying for the Canadian Air Force, I decided that I would join. I really had no idea what the air force would be doing, but I imagined that it would have the most advanced aircraft and that I would be taught the most advanced flying techniques.

However, I joined the Canadian Air Force before if became the *Royal* Canadian Air Force. Later, I became aware that the missing word meant we would be doing anything but *Royal* flying. After we had completed our training, we were told that we had become military pilots. We were all sure there would be a ceremony to give us our wings. The day that we were expecting to receive the details of the graduation, our instructor strutted into the class as he had every other day. Under one arm was a clipboard, as usual; under the other arm was a cardboard box. He walked to the front of the room and threw down the clipboard and the box.

"Fine work boys, you have completed your training. You may not receive your commissions for some time, but you will continue to fly with us for various duties," he said.

We shuffled uneasily in our seats. We were unsure of what the various duties would be.

"Well then, we should get on with it. You will have the rest of the day off. Oh, yes, I nearly forgot. You can come up here and take a couple of these wings in this box."

That was a clear introduction to the kind of role we would hold after our training. There would be no ceremony, no advanced flight training. We would taxi around government officials, carry airmail, and do any work that had to be done. The only difference between the bush pilots and us was that we wore uniforms.

Like the rest of the pilots who were flying for the Canadian Air Force, I had my share of bush flying. I asked for transfers many times to get out of the daily routine of flying menial errands. I thought I was lucky when I received my transfer in 1922 to the Western Provinces. I was sure that the flying would improve.

I was sent to High River, Alberta. The staff at the base was large. There were twenty-two men and eight officers. We walked into the office where we were to receive our first orders. The officer standing at the table called over the five pilots I was with. We walked to the table and looked down at the map that was laid out.

"Gentlemen, we have an important task at hand," he said. I shuffled my weight from one foot to the next, uneasily. I had heard this statement of importance used for the most boring of tasks I had done in the past.

"What do you see gentlemen?" asked the officer as he pointed at the map. We all stepped closer and looked at what he was pointing at. The pointer's tip was at rest on a blank spot on the map.

"You, Fred Wilson, what do you see?" the officer asked.

"Nothing sir. Nothing, but a blank spot on the map," I replied.

"Exactly," replied the officer.

We stood in silence unsure of whether we should laugh or, in military fashion, agree with the statement as though it were very significant. We all responded with knowing nods.

"This area has never been mapped," continued our officer. Again we all nodded. "Our assignment is to photograph the area from the air."

We all stood in silence. Was this going to be the interesting work we all hoped for? None of us had ever been involved in aerial photography before. Maybe this was what we wanted. Pilots who proved to be successful at aerial photography could later get jobs as crop dusters as both required the ability to fly straight lines at a slow and continuous rate. It was not what I was expecting.

After the first day, I realized that I was not really flying the way I wanted to. Flying was taking risks and being free to go wherever you wanted to. I wanted to see how high I could go, how fast could I go, how low and how slow. That was what I wanted to do in the air force.

There was only one solution. I decided to see how much of my kind of flying I could do before I was kicked out of the air force. While I was photographing a section of unknown ground on my second day, I flew up higher and higher until I was above the clouds. Then I put the airplane into the fastest dive I could. I looped around and even went into a spin once.

* * *

I was not surprised when I received notice that the Commanding Officer wanted to see me. The photographs had been processed. Some poor guy was trying to put them together to formulate a map. I walked to the central office, convinced that I was about to be released to civilian life. The Commanding Officer had a reputation for being fair and tough. If he were, I wouldn't be in uniform by noon.

I stepped to the door and knocked.

"Come in!"

"You wanted to see me?" I asked. He stopped for a moment and looked at me.

"Yes, Fred Wilson."

"Yes," I replied in a firm voice. I was ready for this.

"I received your work from yesterday," he said. I stood at attention as he sat down behind his desk. "Sit down, Fred."

I sat down quickly and stared at the officer.

"Do you have anything to say?" he asked.

"No sir," I replied.

"I also watched your flight yesterday. Did you realize that?"

"No sir."

"I was flying behind you."

"Really sir?"

"I have a new transfer for you today."

"That soon sir?"

"I saw what you could do yesterday. We received a request to send a pilot to the British Columbia coast. Would you like to learn how to pilot the flying boats out there?"

"Yes sir," I replied.

"You can take the train this afternoon."

I stood up and saluted. I turned and was gone.

* * *

I couldn't believe the weather on the west coast. It was warm and moist. I loved the smell of the sea after the dry Alberta air. I had a feeling when I arrived that this was finally going to be the place where I could fly the way I had hoped. The flying boats were huge and powerful. I loved the feeling of being in a boat one moment, then in an airplane the next. I think it was the closeness of the water and the slowness of the craft right before takeoff followed by the light feeling of flight that I liked. There was no simple flying here. If we had to do some aerial photography, we would not have to fly in straight lines. The mountains and the bush required constant attention. The flying I liked most involved something more than taxiing people

209

around or surveying the land below. It was police work.

I was on duty in 1923 when a call came from the inspector of fisheries reporting a serious offence.

I stepped into the Royal Canadian Air Force office at Jericho Beach.

"What's the call from the fisheries' officer for?"

"Three American fishermen were fishing illegally in Canadian waters. The fishermen did not respond to the Fisheries' patrol boat called the *Malaspina*. When the Americans tried to get away, the Canadians fired and the other was stopped."

"Why do they need me then?" I asked.

"Let me finish, would you? One of the Americans was killed. The other two sank the boat, but they were picked up by the fisheries' boat. Then, the Americans stole one of the row boats from the *Malaspina* and got away," said the clerk.

"That sounds ridiculous. What did they do, just let the guys walk around the deck of their boat?"

"It looks that way. That's why you have to go look for them. They are on the west side of Vancouver Island. They want you to hurry because they think there is another American ship out there that will pick them up."

"I'm on my way. I hope I can get them. I'll be flying right over the Island."

"Good luck," called the clerk.

This really was what I had hoped to do when I joined the RCAF. I was free to fly as I saw fit. I searched the west coast of Vancouver Island, but the call had come too late for me to find anything. I returned to Jericho Beach. I didn't have to wait too long to get my chance at another call.

* * *

I was doing my regular check on the flying boat. The fuel tank was full. The mechanic said that the engines were ready to go. I was expecting to carry out a routine patrol of the coastline when a man ran up to me and handed me a piece of paper. At a glance, I knew it was an order. I took a quick look at the man again. He was wearing a Canadian customs uniform.

"Jump in!" I said without opening the orders. I made my way into the pilot's seat, then began turning the motor over. In a moment, the motors were at full speed and I was skipping over the water. After I lifted from the water, I leaned over and asked, "What is this all about?"

"You mean you don't know?" asked the man bewildered.

"Did you see me read the orders?" I asked.

"No, but…"

"Don't hold it back, you can tell me what is happening."

"We have a man in a motor boat that has a contraband substance…"

"Right, we have a rum-runner. Am I going in the right direction?"

The man looked out of the window on his side for a moment. "Yes, that's the right direction."

"It's not too large, is it?"

"What?"

211

"The boat we are chasing."

"Oh, it is a small one."

"There it is," I said.

"What? Where?"

"There," I said pointing straight ahead.

"Already? Well now, I guess we are going to have to pull right up to him."

"No problem," I said as I let the airplane down to a level just above the surface of the water. The rumrunner took one look and couldn't believe what he was seeing. There was no way that he could dream of out running us. He slowed right down and stopped. I pulled close and the customs officer shook his head.

"This is where I get off. You can follow and make sure that I don't have any trouble," said the officer.

"Sure."

I circled the boat below the entire way back to port. I was glad that I was on the west coast doing this kind of work. As the different agencies were becoming more certain of our abilities, they called on us sooner than in the past. We stopped a lot of illegal fishing and rum running after that, but another change would end it. The Royal Canadian Air Force the turned strictly to military flying.

25. The Last Big Experiment

The door of the large suburban house opened to reveal a gray-hair man. He stepped back and swept his hand away from the door and toward the interior. The younger man stepped in.

"You are Mr. Bilson," said the old man to the younger.

"Yes."

The pioneer aviator, Ted Walker did not have to be introduced.

"What are writing? A newspaper report?"

"No, a magazine story."

"Oh, yes, a magazine piece. You know I just finished a book on the early days of flying."

"I heard that."

"I am glad that these stories are being told. People don't know enough about the early flights. Well, what was it that you want to write about?"

"The first mail flight across Canada."

213

"Are you talking about Brian Peck's flight of 1918 between Montreal and Toronto?"

"No, the flight from Halifax to Vancouver, or was it Victoria, in 1920."

"That story isn't written about very much."

"That is why I am interested. Who planned the trip? Who was the pilot?"

"The pilot…" said Walker as he leaned back in the chair with a wide smile on his face. "I guess I will have to tell you more before I tell you the name of all the pilots involved."

"There was more than one? Do you mind if I record this?" asked Bilson as he pulled out his tape recorder.

"No, go ahead. Do you know when they finally got a road across this country?"

"No," said Bilson as he spread the tape recorder's mike and wires on the coffee table in front of Walker.

"Not until the 1940s, after the Second World War."

"Oh?"

"Most travel before that was by train. Cars and trucks were still impractical. Airplanes, well, not much was known about them. Well, in the summer of 1920, planes had just crossed the Atlantic and the Rockies. Longer distances were being covered; the Americans had even flown to the Arctic Circle; but no one had flown across the country yet. Some had the idea that an airplane might be faster than a train. People wanted to know if a cross-country flight was possible."

"That's when they decided to carry some mail across the country?"

"No, not really. The mail was considered secondary. I am an amateur philatelist: a collector of rare stamps and envelopes. The mail taken on this first trip was not official airmail because it did not have special postage for the event or a special inked stamp to show the date and place that it was picked up. Those letters were just unmarked envelopes that would otherwise have been sent by rail. There were also letters from one mayor to another to show the stopping points along the way. The pilots signed these envelopes.

"To start with, the flights were planned and sponsored by the Canadian Air Board. There were a couple of trial flights on parts of the route. The first was out of Halifax on July 17, 1920. Two pilots, Colonel Leckie and Captain H. A. Wilson, flew two HS2L flying boats. They hoped to get to Roberval, Quebec by 7 o'clock in the evening on the following day. Later, a second successful flight was made with the same aircraft.

"Captain Wilson took off on August 26, but didn't reach Ottawa until the 28th. The actual flying time, though, was only 14 hours and a few minutes. That was the first time an aircraft had flown from the Atlantic coast to the capital.

"After those first few flights, we knew what to expect. There would be layovers in different communities across the country. The mail wasn't going to be very fast. That is, an airplane could not cross the country as fast as a train because the flight could not be a nonstop tour from coast to coast. It had to be a relay.

215

"There would be some difficulties flying over northern Ontario, because the only place to land was in the water. A seaplane was needed. The aircraft was shipped out by train for that part of the run. Even though the Canadian Air Force supplied the pilots and the planes, everything had to be in civilian colors and the pilots wore civilian clothes.

"As could be expected, there were problems. In this case, it began with the decision to use a Fairley seaplane outfitted in England. The Fairley was to fly from Halifax to Winnipeg. That very seaplane had been fixed up to attempt a trans-Atlantic flight, but as you know, by that time Alcock and Brown had succeeded in doing that.

"Now, this machine had its own bad luck. The Fairley was in Montreal waiting to be transported out to the East Coast when a decision was made to fly it out. Basil Hobbs and Robert Leckie were the pilots to fly that run. Their flight was on October 4th, but just west of Fredericton, New Brunswick the engine wasn't working well. At the same time, a storm forced them to land on the St. John River. The river was flooded. They floated to a bridge, tucked the machine under it like it was a garage, and then started repairs. On October 5th, 1920, they finally got to Halifax at about half past 4 o'clock.

"The next day, the two pilots thought they were ready, but there are some planes, it seems, that decide not to go anywhere —the Fairley was one of those. Because the two pilots couldn't get the airplane to take off with their heavy load, they unloaded some of the cargo. The destination was changed from Winnipeg to

Ottawa. By this time, it was October 7th. There first leg was completed when they landed at Saint John and delivered a letter to the mayor from J.S. Parker, the mayor of Halifax. The Fairley took off in fifteen minutes, heading up the St. John River. It wasn't going to make it though. To the pilots' surprise, the cowling that encased the engine broke away and ripped off an oil pump, covering them in oil and gas. That airplane must have been down on the water in record time.

"You think they were surprised with that, but the situation just got worse. The Fairley just kept sinking until it was on the bottom of the river. The pilots were quickly rescued, but the plane was a complete loss.

"Well, the flight had to go ahead. They requested another airplane from Halifax, one of the old and reliable single-engine HS2L flying boat. With this plane, Hobbs and Leckie were on their way in the afternoon. At ten after 10 o'clock, they arrived at Rivere du Loup, landing in what was a dark storm.

"They needed another aircraft because they had to send the HS2L back to Halifax. The next day, a huge F3 twin-engine flying boat arrived from Montreal. Another airman joined them at this point, Mr. Heath, an air engineer.

"Early in the morning, they were on their way to Ottawa pushing against strong head winds all the way. They arrived at noon.

"After their arrival, there were a few formalities with the greetings of Colonel Redpath and the secretary of the Air Board, J. A. Wilson. I think they picked up another airman, what was his name ... Oh; yes it was Captain Johnson, a navigator.

"Because the route to Winnipeg was uncharted by air, they needed whatever help they could get. They didn't have navigation aids set up like they do today. Even Johnson's help, they had to fly conservatively. The crew followed the Ottawa River to the mouth of the Mattawa, and then they turned west toward North Bay. The pilot had to fly another 250 miles further to Sault Ste Marie. To do this, the crew flew straight out over Lake Nipissing until they reached the delta of the Georgian Bay. They flew close to the north shore of Lake Huron to St. Joseph's Channel and then to Hay Lake. Finally, they landed at Sault Ste Marie at 5 o'clock.

"The three men had traveled a long way, but they wanted to break new trails. The crew prepared to fly at night, a risky act at that time. The pilots planned to fly across Lake Superior during the night, but just as they were taxiing down the river to take off, a fog set in. After deciding that they could not continue in such conditions, they set anchor and slept in the aircraft. Flying would have to wait until sunrise the next day. On October 10th, the plane was in the air on its way to Kenora.

"That part of the flight wasn't eventful. I guess that is what every pilot wishes for. After refueling in a short time at Kenora, they were in the air late in the afternoon on their way to Winnipeg. The pilots decided to land at Selkirk when it began to get dark. Luck must have been with them because as they landed, they narrowly missed a barge in the middle of the river.

"They took the railway to get the Winnipeg mail bag to the city as soon as possible. The next day, they went back to Selkirk, flew their airplane to Winnipeg, and landed on the Red River. At that point, Captain C. W. Cudemore, Captain Hay-Home, and Sergeant Young took over. Leckie and Hobbs traveled by train to Vancouver to meet the plane.

"The new pilots, flying one of the large De Havilland 9's, were off at a few minutes to five in the morning on October 11th. I was working for the Canadian Aircraft Company in Winnipeg at the time. That's why I was there on that cold morning when they took off before dawn. Even going over the Rockies late in the year—I'll tell you, I wasn't sure they were going to make it, but I waved them on.

"Now they were supposed to land at Moose Jaw, but the crew had trouble at half past eight when they were over Regina. They were forced to land in an airfield just outside the city. Well, the back up machine that was kept at Winnipeg as also wrecked. An airplane had to be borrowed from Cudemore and Young at Moose Jaw. Then the two pilots flew right over Moose Jaw instead of landing there. I'll bet there were a lot of disappointed town's folk.

"At Calgary, the next pilot, Captain G. A. Thompson, waited with another De Havilland that had been shipped out west for the run over the mountains. But, the weather prevented Thompson and his co-pilot, Tylee from making an attempt until October 13th. It was just about noon when the biplane took off for Vancouver, traveling by Banff and through the Kicking Horse Pass. Bad weather began to close in and they were forced to land at Revelstoke. The crew was lucky to find a landing field at Sam Crowe's ranch, about three miles south of the community.

"Well, Cudemore and Young had to stay in Revelstoke for a couple of days, but the mayor entertained them.

"They were off again on the 15th of October. That is not to say that is was a clear, warm day. The crew could see clouds pushing toward the west, filling the Eagle Pass, but felt they had to go. The pilots had just gotten into the air when the cloud ceiling fell, creating a thick fog. They had to land at Merritt at a quarter to two in the afternoon. The weather did not get much better on the 17th. The airmen stayed by their machine ready to move on.

"Luckily, there was a small break in the cloud at about eight in the morning. In moments they were on their way down through the Coquihalla Pass. They finally sighted the Fraser River then followed it. As the clouds fell, the plane descended until it was only a few feet above the rushing water of the river. The pilots twisted and turned down the canyons, hoping for the best. They couldn't climb up with the dense clouds laying overhead and the high cliffs on all sides.

"Finally, the storm ended and the town of Agassiz was spotted. They landed nearby for more fuel. Soon, they were back in the air. The Fraser Valley opened up to reveal farmlands marking the way through the hard driving rain. They pushed on past Thompson until they were finally able to land at the Brighouse Park racetrack near Richmond, just outside Vancouver.

"Well, there were the usual honors and banquets, but few people paid attention because the flight had been given little coverage in the newspapers. The flight was pretty good for those days—across the country in forty-five flying hours over ten days.

"After that Tylee and Thompson flew from Vancouver to Victoria. Once that was finished, they shipped all the aircraft back east to Camp Borden by train. The F3 stayed at Winnipeg where it was used for forest patrols and aerial photography."

"And that was the flight?"

"Yes, it was."

"Were there many other experimental flights after that?"

"You mean with how far one could go, how fast?"

"Yes, that's what I mean."

"No, I would have to say that this flight across Canada was the end of the experiments. Better airplanes were needed to do more."

26. A Summer Fair to Remember

My story, the story of those early days when I was flying at summer fairs for a fee, begins with the start of my company; that was in the spring of 1919. I was in Saskatoon when I established a flying service. My name is Stan McClelland. I was with the Royal Flying Corps when it changed to the Royal Air Force in the Great War. I should point out that I was a flying instructor at Beamsville, near Hamilton.

Like many others, I couldn't resist buying my own Curtiss Jenny when the air force sold them at the end of the war. I figured that I had as good a chance as anyone to make money flying. In 1919, I left Ontario with my two Curtiss Jennies. When I got to Saskatoon, I set to work building a hangar. A strip of flat prairie was my runway.

The Curtiss Jenny biplanes had little room for passengers or cargo. Not many thought that a flying service could be profitable. We centered our company

223

on flying at summer fairs for a fee. The biplane was not new, but many people in small towns still couldn't wait to watch them fly. Their questions hadn't change much from the early days. The fairs were so much the same that I forgot who I had met and where I had been. Except there was one fair at a prairie town that I would never forget. It was in Dodsland, Saskatchewan.

I thought the fair would be routine. When I arrived with my Jenny, I saw that my helper, a fellow named Spooner was already waiting for me. He was a good mechanic and very helpful. The Ford truck he was driving had tools and more important, tanks of fuel and oil. I had flown enough to know that many of these small communities did not have high-grade gas and oil. Since most farmers still used steam tractors and horses, the need for fuel and motor oil was limited.

Well, we arrived on June 16, 1920, a beautiful clear day. I was soon introduced to the leading citizens of the community: Charles Henderson and Florence MacKenzie. Henderson came to Saskatchewan in 1909 from Newport, Nebraska. He found work with the Luseland Development Company. Henderson wanted to create a settlement. He organized a group of new friends to buy ten sections of land here. In 1913, when the Grand Trunk Railway came through the area, the place really picked up. Henderson later set himself up as the publisher of the local paper called *The Prairie Times*. He also became the secretary of the school board, a member of the hospital board, a real estate agent, an insurance agent and a land developer and a farmer. Now, Miss MacKenzie was the teacher in the town. From the comments I heard, everyone was expecting them to announce their wedding date soon.

The two brought me into the office of *The Prairie Times* for what I thought would be an interview for the newspaper. The room had just the bare essentials of a typewriter and a simple press in the back.

"How can I help you?"

"We understand that you can take passengers with you in your biplane," said Charles.

"Yes, two." He gets to the point fast, I thought. No introductions, straight into the interview. I liked that.

"How many bags could you carry with two extra passengers?" asked Florence.

"Well, probably two medium sized bags." That was an odd question. Usually, interviewers are just interested in my show.

"That will do," said Charles quickly.

"Excuse me?" I asked.

"Well, we want to be married."

"Yes," I replied.

"We don't want to wait for all the formalities. We want to get on with it."

"Oh?"

"We couldn't stay around the town after getting married without inviting everyone in town. People here would think we were quite rude," said Florence.

"Really?"

"We have a plan."

"It includes me flying you somewhere to be married, maybe elope?"

"That's half right," said Charles.

"We have no way of knowing how long it would take to find a chapel and a minister in a strange city like Saskatoon," said Florence.

"True," I said.

"Well, the Reverend Challis lives in the back of *The Prairie Times*."

"The ceremony is already arranged?" I asked.

"Will you do it?"

"Of course," I said. "But, what about the fair?"

"The community can't be suspicious. You have to go out and do your show while we get ready. When you land, come here while your helper gets ready for the flight to Saskatoon."

"You do have it all figured out…"

"Just wait a moment, Stan. That's your name isn't it?"

"Yes."

"Well then, Stan, I must ask you if you would act as best man."

"I would be honored," I said. I stood up and left. I knew that I had to fly the show as if nothing was happening.

After the show, I made my way to *The Prairie Times*. I told Spooner that there would be two bags at the newspaper office to put in the Jenny. He was not to let anyone see what he was doing. He grinned and nodded.

"Hurry," said Charles as he stood with Florence and the bridesmaid, Nina MacKenzie.

"Do you think that they know anything?"

"They might," I said. "They were talking a lot when I came here."

"Quickly now," said Florence.

That was the fastest marriage I had ever seen. Reverend Challis said very quickly, "Do you take this man as your husband?"

"I will."

"Do you take this woman to be your wife?"

"Yes, now hurry they're figuring this out."

We all ran out without handshakes. There was maybe a little kiss between the two newly weds; I can't remember. We ran to the waiting car that took us to the Jenny as fast as Charles could drive the mile out onto the prairie. I could swear I saw several cars in hot pursuit. We were soon in the biplane and lifting off the ground.

* * *

There was a write-up about it in the Saskatoon *Daily Star* on June 18th. I have it right here: "The first airplane elopement in the history of Western Canada, took place at the little town of Dodsland, Sask., Wednesday night, when, with Lieutenant H. S. McClelland, Saskatoon aviator, in the guise of a be goggled and leather-coated Don Cupid, and with the propeller whirring a Lorengrin hum, Charles A. Henderson, one of Dodsland's biggest farmers and land operators, lifted his bride, formerly Miss Florence McKenzie into the forward cockpit of McClelland's Curtiss plane and zoomed away on a honeymoon trip into cloud land."

The reporter explained that he found, "The bride … toying with a Denver sandwich in a Second Avenue

227

café when seen by the writer. 'I'm still up in the air,' was all she said…"

Then, the *Winnipeg Tribune* reported on June 20th, that, "the whole town had been waiting for the event for months, and had planned to celebrate the affair in typical western manner." The scene was drawn in color when the reporter wrote that "the couple race for the auto, the towns people aboard scores of other autos and started in hot pursuit, commandeering bags of rice from the stores as they go; the eloping couple race up to a waiting airplane; they leap aboard; the pursuing cars are only a few rods behind; the propeller starts to whirl, the plane skims over the prairie as the first pursuer whirls alongside then up in the air amid a barrage of rice!"

After their trip to Winnipeg, the couple returned to Dodsland to continue their lives. I heard, Mrs. Henderson continued to teach in Dodsland. Mr. Henderson defeated William Herridge in the election of 1940. He represented the Kindersley constituency in Ottawa from 1940 to 1945 as a Liberal.

That was the one story from 1920 that I remember well.

27. Sealing With a Biplane

I am Captain Roy Grundy. Before I was a pilot I was a skipper on a sealing ship. Sealing in Newfoundland was a tradition that went back to the 1800s. There were ways of sealing with dangers equal to any other we fishermen knew. Of course, we had to do what we had to do. Sealing was an important source of income for us. If there was any way to get to St. John's where the sealing vessels were at port each spring, we went. We tried to get onto one of the sealers late in the winter. If you had a good start on the season by getting a good bit of money from sealing, the saying was that you would have a profitable summer. Because of this superstition, no one wanted to change the way the traditional hunt was carried out.

Well, I was a young man in the 1920s when someone had an idea; airplanes could be flown over the ice fields, spot the herds of seals and tell the sealers where to find them. Well, no one wanted to do that. On the ice, sealers would set out in large sealing ships to look for the herds. The sealers would take shifts up in the crow's nest with field glasses, looking. When the skipper saw a herd, he pushed into the ice to get there.

The first I heard of a biplane scouting out herds of seals was in 1921. Sidney Cotton and Bennett worked for the Aerial Survey Company in St. Johns. These men convinced the owners, not the skippers, that the idea was a good one.

The original plan had huge obstacles to overcome. The flights were very long, about 350 miles, because they had to start out on the land then fly back. It wasn't surprising when the carburetors and the radiators froze up so that the men couldn't get their machines into the air for months. That was the end of that idea. The sealing season is very short. By the time the airplanes were up in the air getting reports about where the herds were, the ice had broken up and the seals had taken to the sea.

I guess the effort wasn't lost as far as the pilots were concerned. They found out what it took to fly the aircraft in harsh conditions. The pilots had next year to prove that their idea could work except none of the sealers believed for a moment that they would ever be able to spot and report the location of seals before the end of the season.

In March 1922, the biplanes were flying again. This time it was early enough to spot seals for the hunt. From what I heard, the pilots took their planes out there and found some herds, but the owners were now as uncertain as the sealers were. The company didn't have a contract with them. By the time the owners had signed with the pilots, the tide and currents had changed and it was too late too catch the seals.

In 1923, I was a pilot from Newfoundland who had a better idea of how to do use a biplane to find the seal herds. I had been in the Royal Air Force and a seal skipper. I hoped that would make a difference to the skippers I was trying to work for. My idea was to carry the plane on the ship. When the opportunity arose, the crew could lower the machine over the side, and then I would fly out to circle the area. The biplane had to be small enough to be carried on the ship and to use a short take off area. A plane they called the Baby Avro was ideal. I had a small 80-horse power engine in it. The English A. V. Roe Company Ltd supplied the Avro and its pilot.

The machine was put on the *S.S. Neptune* after I convinced the ship owners in St. Johns, the Job Brothers and Company Ltd, and the Bowing Brothers. The skipper and the salty old fishermen on the *Neptune* were not convinced and that was the core of my difficulties. It didn't matter that I was a skipper of a sealer before because as far as they were concerned, anyone who wanted to change the tradition of the hunt was not much of a sealer.

The skipper was the one who had to allow the English pilot to fly. He had to order the men to untie the Avro and lower it to the ice. The trouble was that we found small herds here and there. As long as there was a small group of seals to hunt, the sealers didn't need the biplane. The skipper had to feel desperate. In 1923, we did exactly what the other fishermen did on the ship. The airplane did not fly that season.

231

I hoped that the next season would not be so easy for the skippers. The advantages of using a biplane would be recognized if the machine could go up and bring back news.

Of course, the skippers and the fishermen complained to the owners about the biplane. I had some real negotiating to do to get the owners to allow me to try one more time the next season. Since the operation wasn't costing the owners much, they allowed me to take another run at it in March 1924 on the *S.S. Eagle*.

This time, my luck had changed. That year, I was the pilot. My English friend from the A.V. Roe Company hadn't liked his duties the year before. More important, the skipper was much more interested in the idea.

"You're going to patrol for seals, are you?" asked the skipper.

"It should be a significant breakthrough in sealing," I said.

"There is only one way to do the sealing," said a fisherman who was passing by.

"You figure it will be that easy?"

"There should be no problems."

"There are always problems," said the skipper.

"Like breaking ice for the entire season without a single seal?"

"Like bringing that machine down on the ice if the fog drops as fast as it takes for a whale to spout."

"Yeah."

"It should be interesting. After we can't find a seal for days, when the men are unsettled, we can put a show on for them," said the skipper.

"That is an idea."

I was relieved. The skipper would not stubbornly keep his men in the crow's nest and refuse to allow the biplane down on the ice like the year before. H. E. Wallis, my engineer and I were hopeful, but we had seen good will before only to have it turn bad as soon as we set to sea.

True to his word, we had been only in the ice for a few days without a sighting, when I was called over to the side of the ship where the skipper was looking out on a icescape was flat as I had ever seen.

"Well, Roy, what do you think?"

"It's a cold day," I replied.

"I mean, the ice."

"It's flat, flat enough to take off."

"Why not try it? There's no reason to keep our trump card up our sleeves. Let's see that machine fly."

"Okay."

"This is your idea. All I did was say yes."

"Sure."

Away we went, calling the grudging crew to untie the Avro and put her over the side. I was nervous as the men worked. There was not a single interested worker among them. Some of the men had to clean the runway a little so that I could get a start.

I took along Jabze Windsor, the Master Watch on the ship. It wasn't long before we had sighted a herd of some 125,000 seals. In 35 minutes, we were back at the ship with news. The *Eagle* was easy to find because of the smoke pouring out of the steam boiler's fire. The catch was so massive that I had made many believers of the fishermen on board.

Soon after, the ice began to break up. Wallis and I removed the skis on the biplane and placed floats on the under carriage. The skipper said we could go ahead with one more flight. We jumped into the Avro, then tried to take off, but there was so much vibrating that we gave up. That night ice and fog closed in. The season was over for us.

Since I wasn't able to go back to flying for the sealing ships in 1925, a new pilot, Jack Caldwell, went out with the Baby Avro on the *Eagle*. From what I heard the same skipper and many of the crew did not return the next season. Caldwell had the same old problems. The crew refused to believe that the biplane was of any value for sealing. They generally believed that the stories of the year before had been fabricated and exaggerated. One fact remained the same. The observations from the crow's nest were based heavily on luck, and in 1925, luck was not with the *Eagle's* skipper. Out of desperation, they lowered the Avro onto the ice and sent Caldwell off. He saw that the ship was sailing in the wrong direction. The ship's direction was changed to meet the main herd, but there was some distance to travel before the *Eagle* reached the spot. After two days, they had not yet found the herd. The biplane was grudgingly lowered onto the ice once more. Again, the pilot found the main herd. Soon, the ship met it and took in a full catch.

This time more skippers and fishermen believed the stories. More important though, the Bowering

Brothers Company noticed the results. The same situation occurred again in 1926 and 1927 with one exception: the Avro was in the air much sooner on the voyage. Finally, many more believed in using a plane when the ship owned by the Bowering Brothers got the top record for catches.

After the success of air observations in 1927, Caldwell got a new, larger plane, an Avro Avian. This machine was able to fly 500 miles in one circuit. That was just the beginning. The climax came in 1928 when flying stations and bases were established on the coasts of Newfoundland, Labrador, the Gulf of the St. Lawrence, and on Anticosti Island. Caldwell had to supply information on where the seals were for the ships. The sealing company decided that it needed to know more about the migration of seals. Up to that time, the sealers had been sailing blind. They had no idea of where the seals were or where they would be moving during the various parts of the season. With extensive flying that year, Caldwell mapped the migration.

Before any ship left port that season, Caldwell already knew where they should go and what size of herd they could expect when they got there. Using this information, the skippers sailed straight to the seal grounds, took their catch, and returned so fast that they were, for the first time ever, able to return to the ice for a second cargo.

In 1929, pilot Alex Harvey replaced Jack Caldwell. He continued to do the same work as Caldwell had done the year before, but the risks of winter flying caught up with him. Harvey was caught in the air when a heavy fog settled in. The Avro Avian was wrecked in his blind landing at St. Anthony.

With this, the practice of using the Avro was over. For different reasons, the story of the seal pilots was also over. The sealing company had enough knowledge about the migration of the seals by 1929 that the flights no longer added little new information. At the same time, that year marked the beginning of the Great Depression. The ship companies decided that they could no longer afford the air service.

The airplane dramatically changed the sealing industry in such a short time that it is amusing to think of those first flights when the fishermen and skippers were certain that it would not be useful.

28. Gliding to Fame

Some have called my work in the area of flying, or should I say gliding, a bit crazy. I should tell you that I'm Norman Bruce. By the time I was fifteen, I thought I was old enough to take to the air. Now, since there was no way that I could get an airplane or even much of a ride in someone else's aircraft, I planned to build my own machine. Unfortunately, there wasn't much to build with on our farm at Medicine Hat, Alberta in 1922. The solution I came up with was to build a sailplane. As far as that goes, my father didn't take the sailplane too seriously either. To him, it was just a big kite that would probably never fly. He was half right.

Working from pictures in magazines and whatever information I could find out about aircraft construction, I set to work on a sail plane that looked more like a kite than anything else. I had to run to launch the craft while hanging on by my armpits. As a safety precaution, which was more of an attempt to make it look like a biplane, I put on a set of wheels.

It took me two years to build the plane with wood, cotton and canvas. When it was nearly finished, I had to cover the wings with something that would seal it. Boat varnish was all I could find around the farm. Of course, it sealed the wings fine, but it really added to the weight. I didn't really know that would have much of an effect. It seemed to me that the wings were kind of magic. They could carry anything into the air if they were the right shape and sealed. I had never had a chance to look at a real airplane, but that didn't stop me.

The glider was ready to fly in the summer of 1924. I carried it to the top of a hill then ran down. I was sure that all I needed to make it fly was lots of speed. I could feel the weight of the glider lifting, but it hadn't taken off. I remember Dad watching with this broad grin. He thought it was something to see a kid putting a machine together like that and expecting it to fly.

I worked at running faster and faster until one day it happened! I was running down the hill as fast as I could when a breeze hit the wings and up I went. I was lifted only a few feet, but it felt great. Now I knew that I would succeed if I ran into the wind. I carried the sailplane back to the farmyard. I knew what my Dad would say when I got there.

"Well, son did you take to the air today?"

"I did, I really did it today."

"Really? You go clear across the field?"

"No, not that far; just a few feet, but it really happened."

"Oh?" he said. I could tell that he believed me. He could believe I flew a few feet. A few yards would have made a real tale!

"It was because of the wind. A breeze came up when I ran down the hill. That's the trick, I have to wait for a wind and I will be up."

"You think you can fly well enough to do that?"

"Sure."

"Whatever," he said with a shrug. He probably thought that if I had to work this hard to fly just a few feet; a real wind would only give me a couple yards. I guess he was right.

Tomorrow if it is windy, I will fly for the longest flight possible, I thought. I had to face right into the wind, then let it go. I wished the hardest wind of the summer would come the next day. It came! The problem was that it came in the early morning. The plane flew very well except for one problem: I wasn't piloting it. The wind picked it up high enough to bring it down in the farmyard in a million pieces.

Well, I set straight to work on the next plane. That last flight was enough to make me want to fly. The progress was much faster than the first one because I had experience. Construction was well underway when word traveled to the men at the local air station that I was a crazy kid building my own airplane. An officer arrived at the farm, introduced himself and asked to see what I had done. I told him about the first plane and the second. He was taken aback when I said, "Yes, that's right. I used the varnish for boats." Dad was there listening to the conversation. Once we finished looking the new project over, he turned to Dad and said, "If anyone can tell him not to fly this thing it would be you."

"Why is that?" asked Dad.

"Well, it is heavy and not very safe."

"Oh?"

"I would say that the biggest problem is that an aircraft truly needs wings; real wings," he said.

"We can't afford all that fancy varnish and glue you probably think we need."

"Well, that would be an improvement, but there is a more basic improvement that I would suggest, even if you don't use the materials we would use at the station. The wings have to be over twenty feet from one tip to the next."

"Twenty feet?" I said. I had never thought it would have to be that big to fly.

"And maybe you would like a little control of the machine."

"What?"

"Rudders, you need flaps and rudders to control the flight."

"You can control these machines in the air?"

The officer laughed loudly.

"Look, I'll take you to the station and show you how airplanes are put together. You're going to persist no matter what, I can see that, but you need a much better idea of what you're doing."

"That's great," I said.

Soon, I was out at the station looking at every airplane they had. I tried all the controls. Finally, I was given just what I wanted: a flight.

The rest of the summer was spent building a sail plane with a 22 foot wing span with no rudder, but there were flaps to get up and down a bit better (after all that was what I was hoping to do). The new plane was also large enough to have a wicker chair in it. In 1928, I had a machine that could be pulled behind a truck.

Soon, I was flying. It was short lived, though; I had only three good flights before I had a bumpy landing that finished off the glider.

Well, it wasn't long before I was old enough to go to the United States for an aeronautical engineering course. When I got back to Medicine Hat in 1930, I formed a new club called the Cloud Rangers Gliding Club. My two brothers had also qualified for their pilot licenses. Of course, we all set to work on the gliders for the club. But then, my brother had an accident worse than I had ever thought possible. He attempted a takeoff over a cliff, but found himself in a dive straight down. There was no motor and no way to get out of it. None of us ever wore parachutes–they really didn't have a good parachute available in 1930 anyway. The club died with him. The local residences were very unhappy with us at that point.

Yet, even after that tragedy, I just couldn't stop flying. I talked to everyone I could about flying. I found support in an unlikely place. The local women apparently weren't as shaken by the crash as the men had been. That's why we decided to form the Skylarks Gliding Club. There were two ladies who could really fly well. They were Mrs. Ellick and Patricia Terril.

By 1934, we had a new idea. James Fretwell, who was with the Settler Gliding Club, Paul Pelletier, who was flying out of Calgary, and myself got together and formed the Canadian Gliding Boosters. The idea was to take the gliders to the summer fairs. In the years past, biplanes drew a crowd at the summer fairs, but now they were commonplace. We hoped that the new spectacle would be gliders. We planned a trip across the west, including stops at summer fairs to fly for donations.

We set out on May 25, 1935 in a car with the glider in a trailer behind. We stopped in twenty-two different communities from Calgary to Winnipeg to fly the glider. We used the model T to pull the glider into the air. The people were very interested in the flights as gliding was a new curiosity. We completed 410 flights in some of the windiest conditions I could ever remember. There were days we flew when we didn't think it was too wise, but we went ahead anyway.

Because this was during the Great Depression, we couldn't ask for ticket money or we wouldn't have a chance to fly at any summer fairs, but we did hope for the best. The donations from the public weren't that good. We collected $214 in all.

Near the end of the tour, one night after we set the tent up and prepared to wait out the windy conditions, the gusts became worse until suddenly we heard a whip and crack. It was the glider. We ran out, looked around for a moment and realized that the glider was gone. The next morning, it was nothing more than tiny sticks. We gathered as much of the rigging as we could find. What was left of our glider fit easily into a small box.

That was the end of gliding in the early days for me. We were nearly broke. The sport had to wait until the end of the Second World War for me to return to it.

29. Searching for Mystery Gold

Now when I tell you this story, you have to remember that I am only going to tell you what I was told. It is hard, at times, to remember that it happened in 1926. I am not really just making this up. The most bizarre part of the story, the old prospector, Benedict (at least I think that was his name) was a real character.

Old Ben arrived in Calgary with a big promise —a promise for the right kind of investors. Now, old Ben was a rough unshaved surveyor who was more comfortable paddling his canoe on a remote lake in the north, hoping to find a comfortable bank to build a fire on and cook a little food in an old coffee tin than sitting in a small greasy café in the city. How he found the mineral developers, I don't know.

He was walking around the city, but he knew who the mining developers were and where they lived and where they dined. I heard a number of stories about how he got the attention of these men, but the one I like the most was that he just stood there, outside the fancy restaurant they ate at, then went over to them when they came out, calling them by name. The well-dressed men of some means thought they had a bum on their hands, but old Ben figured on that and said quickly, "I have something to show you!" He dug deep into his pocket, pulled out a handkerchief and unwrapped a large nugget of gold. Now, most men who make their living off mining and developing usually don't have a clue what to look for when they are presented with a piece of ore, but there was one thing that they could identify, no matter how little they knew, and that was gold.

Well, Ben got the reaction he figured he would. "Where did you get that?" the financier asked Ben, as if the prospector was just full of dumb glee to tell anyone who asked.

At the right price he would give the developer, Edwards, I think his name was, the information he wanted. Now, you have to understand that at that time in Calgary, and in Canada in general, there was a high rolling attitude. Some people were investing in the stock market and making lots of money. Others were taking all kinds of risks investing in and developing mines that were long shots. After the First World War, everyone wanted prosperity and development.

Well, the businessman agreed to the split of profits as Ben asked for. To find the gold and to mine it, the Northern Syndicate Limited was formed. Edwards needed the most important piece of information from Ben—that was, where was the gold. Ben said, "Where's a map?" It took only a moment for an assistant to rush into the office with the most up-to-date maps of the north. It was a map that sketched in areas of the Yukon, the Mackenzie Valley up to the most northern point at the Bering Straight. The map had an outline of the Great Slave Lake. East of the lake, there were all the landmarks known in the region: none. To be exact, the map showed nothing more than a white plain. Ben looked at the map for a moment and said; "I thought they had mapped more than this. I figured that the map I had was just a little too old."

"What do you mean mapped before?" said Edwards.

"Just that. Probably because no one has been where I was. That's why the gold hasn't been found yet."

"Well, where on this map do you figure the *find* was?"

"Right here," said Ben as he put his finger down on the white plain of the map, east of the Great Slave Lake.

"How are we going to find an ore deposit that is located there?"

"I figure that would be a problem so I marked the area with a cross cut out of the bush. It is by a large lake that is not even on this map. It stands out on the land well, unmistakable. There is a small cabin close by in the clearing. That is where my Indian wife is. She's watching the *find* until I get back."

"How are we supposed to find a mark cut in the bush?"

"Some years ago when I was at a summer fair, I saw one of those biplanes. Well, I paid my dime and took a ride. Have you ever done that? Go up in a biplane?"

"No."

"You can see every detail of the land as clear as could be. Well, that was where I got the idea. You could get an airplane and fly it straight out east from the Great Slave Lake. With a little looking, you should be able to find the mark from the air."

Mr. Edwards began to smile. He had been prepared for the slow process of sending a crew up with the prospector, then waiting a whole year just to get exact information on the location. Now he had all the answers. A thought occurred to the financier. He could quickly find the ore deposit using a small aircraft, start a mining operation, and then be flying gold out of the north by next summer. The idea seemed strange — flying gold out of the bush, but it would work; it could be the way of the future.

Soon after the plan had been laid, fate intervened. Calgary at that time could best be described as a dusty town, but for a prospector who had seen little more than bush and wild animals, it was a scene to behold. Added to Ben's excitement were the signed deal and the money in his pocket. He was ready to celebrate.

Only a matter of hours after his new deal, Ben was in a saloon. As it turned out, too much celebrating wasn't the best idea. Ben was drunk. He was soon in a tussle. It would have been just another swinging night if the two had just used their firsts and nothing else, but Ben was knocked over the head with a bottle. It cracked his skull.

Edwards received word of the events the next day. Ben was not conscious again for some time. Edwards arrived in the hospital room to talk to Ben.

"How are you feeling?"

"Bad, I really got it."

"I have heard." Ben stared at the businessman for a moment. "You do remember who I am, right?"

"Yes."

"You remember the deal we had."

"Sure," said Ben. The businessman looked relieved.

"We will be on our way as soon as you are out of here."

"Sure, that sounds all right. What lake did you want to go fishing in?"

"Fishing, that's funny. I guess we can fish in your lake up in the unmapped regions."

"My lake?"

"You're joking, right? You know that we have a deal?"

"Deal?"

"The ore *find*."

"What?"

"Remember," pleaded Edwards. Ben shook his head. "Gold, you have to remember the gold."

"I'm tired," said Ben.

"Yes, that's it, you need time to recover. You need sleep to help your memory."

With that Edwards left, unsure if the operation to find the gold would go as well as he had hoped. He wasn't going the waste time, not with that sizable nugget of gold on display in his office. That would

249

keep him at it. First, he needed an airplane that could land on water and fly without any support from stations along the way. Edwards didn't know much about airplanes, but he knew the stories of long flights were about the troubles and the repairs needed to keep the biplanes in the air. When he heard about the successes of the Vickers Viking Mark IV, he knew it was the machine he was looking for.

The particular Viking that was for sale had already proved it could fly into the north and return with few problems. The Lauretide Air Service first employed the Viking amphibious flying boat in 1924 for a 900-mile trip in Northern Ontario to deliver treaty payments to natives. The flying time was twelve days. With traditional hiking and canoeing, the trip would have taken most of the summer. In 1925, a group of Americans who had organized a mining syndicate bought the Viking to bring supplies up to Wrangell, Alaska. However, for the most part, the Viking was used in northern British Columbia to prospect, supply, and map blank areas of the map. They mapped areas that had peaks of 10,000 feet. The airplane was used for just about everything up north without the mishaps that were common to other aircraft at the time.

Now, for some unknown reason, the Viking was taken apart, and then sent to the shops of the Ontario Air Service. That is where the Calgary syndicate found the machine and bought it. The aircraft was still in pieces when it was shipped by train to Edmonton.

The men decided to completely overhaul the engine when they were getting it ready. The repairs and overhaul were completed in a month. The pieces were shipped on a train to Lac la Biche on June 16, 1926. The small crew that worked for the Syndicate took all the pieces to one place by the lake to assemble it. The whole operation of putting the plane together took six days. They were ready for a test flight on June 22. They decided to fly from Lac la Biche to Fort Fitzgerald. The two airmen in charge of flying the Viking were Caldwell and Vachon.

Caldwell smiled as he pushed the throttle forward. He heard the newly installed Napier engine whine loudly. It was ready to go.

"We can get the airplane loaded for take off tomorrow morning," said Vachon.

"Can't we make it today?"

"No time, there wouldn't be any point in taking chances now."

"We will have our flight tomorrow then."

"Sounds good to me."

The test flight was not a test flight at all, but the first hop in the run to the north. At the Fort Fitzgerald, they joined the prospecting party of Bill and William, who had arrived by steam riverboat. They would try to find the allusive cross, chopped in the bush.

* * *

They began their summer of flying by establishing caches in the north, flying into that great unmapped region to find a large lake at 61 degrees 30 minutes North and 107 degrees 30 minutes West, to be exact.

The group of four sat down and drank their coffee by the campfire.

"Hey William what do you think about Benedict's story?" asked Bill.

"Can't say. I know a lot of prospectors who go looking for the big *find* discover it. Others have had too much time in the bush…"

"Well, we can start tomorrow by making wider circles around this lake to see what else is around. Then, we will move on to search all the lakes we find until we are sure there are no crosses cut out of the bush," said Caldwell.

"Maybe we should look for smoke. Ben did say he left his woman behind."

"We can look for anything that looks interesting. I would like to stop if there are any people living out here to find out what they know about Ben or his wife."

"That sounds fine to me," said Vachon.

The prospectors agreed. They were going to be busy testing the rock to see if there was anything of interest around.

"Hey, William, what do you think we should name this lake."

"Name the lake?"

"Yes, name it."

"We will have to map it. We need a name on it."

"Why don't we name it after the one who got us in here," said Vachon.

"You mean Ben?"

"No, Caldwell."

Caldwell sat back grinning at the suggestion.

"That sounds good to me," said Bill.

"That's it, Lake Caldwell," said Vachon.

"Hey, wait a moment," said Caldwell.

"We all agreed," said William. "You are outvoted. We will start mapping Lake Caldwell tomorrow."

They were on one of the highest pieces of land in the territories, with an altitude of 1,300 feet above sea level. The water that was flowing off from the lake either flowed north to the Arctic seas or south and east to the Hudson Bay.

The flights were daily with the men flying into many unseen areas in the north. On some occasions, they flew as far as 200 miles further north, where there were lots of rocks but little else. The pilot and his assistant were very careful with their navigation so that they could find their way back. There was no chance of rescue after being lost. They never saw any cross in the bush or any signs of human habitation.

In mid-August, the men realized that they would not be able to continue much longer. The nights were becoming very cold. Thin ice was forming on the lake. They decided to stop their search. The airmen all loaded onto the Viking and flew to Edmonton and then to High River, Alberta. They flew down there on September 4th, landing the machine on solid *terra ferma*. That was the first time an amphibious aircraft landed on solid ground in Canada. The Viking was taken apart in High River where it remained disassembled until 1928 when B. Lundy, who was working between Vancouver and Calgary, bought the aircraft.

They never knew whether the old prospector was telling the truth about the gold in the bush or about his wife who was supposed to be living there somewhere.

The syndicate never found the gold. The prospector, Benedict never returned to the north either.

30. An Early Sailplane

Now, as far as I know, we were one of the first with a sailplane on the prairies. Of course, there were those who were flying gliders: a little plane that looked like an oversized kite with the pilots dangling from the bottom or a little machine with a wicker seat that was gently pulled into the air for a minute or two. In North Battleford, Charles Weber, my brother and I built a sailplane that looked like a modern bush plane with the wind over the top. It had a covered cockpit and a full set of controls.

By 1927, we had heard a lot about the flying that the German glider pilots had done and decided that we could build our own sailplane it we wanted to. Of course, we didn't have any experience with this type of construction. We built the sailplane by hand. It took a year to build. By 1928, we were ready to try the plane out.

"Well, Fred, do you want to try this out?" asked Charles.

"Sure, I'm ready to go." We stood out in the field beside the sailplane and the Chevrolet touring car.

"Are you sure of yourself?"

"Yes, I'll be fine. After all, we have the entire field to fly over."

"And those trees over there, and over there."

"I'm not too worried," I said as I looked around.

I hadn't considered the trees before. I hoped that the controls on the plane worked well enough to either go around or over them. We had done all we could to get the plane as light as possible, but maybe that wasn't enough.

I agreed to take the first flight. The sooner I did it, the sooner we would have our answers. I was lucky that the little roadster didn't have enough power to put me up too high —I needed practice.

I jerked back in the seat as the rope tightened between the sailplane and the car, and then we picked up speed very quickly. The plane jumped and jostled this way and that. That was the roughest ride I ever had until suddenly it began to smooth out. The wings were up off the ground. I couldn't believe it when the aircraft left the ground and rose above the heavy cloud of dust that the car was kicking up. In a moment, I released the pulling rope. I was flying faster than the car below, which disappeared quickly under me. I was flying on my own. The sailplane responded well. I lifted higher as I flew over hot air rising off the field below and carrying me higher.

The trees were approaching, but they were well below the plane. When I dipped one wing and pushed the rudder with my feet, the machine turned nicely. In a moment, I was gliding back to the field the car was on. The roadster looked small. I circled one more time, pushed the nose of the glider down and came in for a bumpy landing.

"You just kept getting higher!" said Charles.

"It's the field; there is hot air rising off it."

"Really?"

"You can go up now," I said.

He was off. It seemed to me that all we did that summer was fly that sailplane. It wasn't that long before we were looking to fly higher and longer. We were averaging 150 to 200 feet high and several minutes of flight. To do better, than that we needed more rope, more power and a longer runway. We lengthened the towrope to 2,000 feet and used an eight-mile runway that was free of wires and flat. We had a truck pull the plane at top speed (that is top speed for eight miles).

Well by the end of the summer, we reached a height of 500 feet staying up for fifteen to twenty minutes at a time. We were always interested in flying after that.

The glider was eventually sent to the Western Development Museum. Now, I hear it is on display in Moose Jaw. Who would ever think that clumsy looking sailplane actually reached 500 feet?

31. Lost on the Atlantic

I am Flying Officer Lewis. I remember that in 1927 we didn't know much about what was in the eastern arctic, but we did know about what was needed to work in the high north and to fly in very cold conditions. For the most part, we knew how well the airplane worked for mapping regions of unknown territories. Many of the areas in the northwest already had been mapped using airplanes right after the First World War. The Canadian government considered these factors when it decided that accurate maps of the Hudson Straight were needed so that ships could navigate the waters of the Hudson Bay. The region and its ice conditions had to be studied before that could happen. The Hudson Bay was going to be a new port for shipping grain from the prairies instead of the slower St. Lawrence River.

This came about because William Lyon Mackenzie King was re-elected as Prime Minster in 1926. His policy for private rail construction was to not have a policy at all. Any private railroad company could build any stretch of rail they thought would be profitable. Well, in a short time, many projects were under construction. The plan to build a railway to the Hudson Bay with Churchill, Manitoba as a northern terminal was one of these projects. Our job was to find a way for the ships to get into the Bay.

In the summer of 1927, ships moved into the Hudson Straight with prefabricated buildings including a radio station and lodging. The expedition was well planned with men to fly and men to make observations about the weather.

Because we had a large area to survey, we had three posts, one each at Nottingham Island, Wakeham Bay, and Port Burwell, which was at the most northern point of Ungava Bay.

In these areas, there were sudden fogs and severely cold conditions. We even experienced dense black fog rise off the water. Our planes had a covered compartment for the cargo or passengers, but the pilots often had to fly in open cockpits. There were enough cases of frostbite to keep our doctor busy.

The story that I remember began on February 17, 1928 when I was flying out of the base at Port Burwell. We had lost several days because heavy, strange fogs kept us on the ground. We were willing to fly in any small opening that came, hoping that the fogs didn't roll in and make us land blind. We had an opportunity a little before noon. A sergeant and an Inuit named Bobby Anakatok and I, Flying Officer Lewis, usually called "Jaggs," were in the air. Our objective was to make it to Baffin Island. We were to fly out to Resolution Island then, after spotting an outcrop, we were to turn, but the fog closed in. We could only guess where the mark had been. We used the compass to set a course for Burwell.

As if that wasn't enough trouble, the engine began to make a rough noise that became louder. I could feel the power and speed drop when I thought I saw dark markings to the port side. I turned the machine in that direction then flew for about fifteen minutes. I must have been off course because the landscape looked like we were near Akpatok Island, which was at the center of Ungava Bay. That made me feel better because I had intentionally flown the airplane in an exaggerated line after I left Resolution so that I would be at the center of Ungava Bay to avoid being lost over the flowing ice packs of the Atlantic. I was sure that I was flying straight toward Burwell now. I hoped that the plane would hold together long enough to make it there. At about 3 o'clock in the afternoon, I still couldn't see any land. Our airplanes had a radio in it. We sent a radio message to the base saying we were over Ungava Bay and had to bring the machine down. Then, I prepared for the worst and brought the nose of the airplane down. The machine bumped hard on the ice. There was a cracking sound as we stopped. I looked around for a minute. There was only an endless sea of cliffs and drifts. I got out of the cockpit. Terry was looking at the damage.

"Well, what does it look like?" I asked.

"Prop is damaged." Terry said as he walked from the front of the craft to the back. "The undercarriage took a bad hit too. It will need some work on both to take off."

"Do you think we will make it out of here any time soon?" asked Bobby.

"Why?" I asked.

"This doesn't look like Ungava. I don't think we should stay here too long."

"What?"

"The ice looks dangerous."

I looked around. I couldn't believe the size of the drifts, ridges, and crevices.

"We better stay here for the night, there isn't much time left anyway."

"That sounds good to me. I could use some food and sleep," said Terry.

No one was looking forward to striking out across the ice the next morning, but we all had a sense that we had to move. I was uneasy because we were on a moving ice flow.

The next morning there was nothing to see. There had been a heavy fall of snow the night before. I hoped to have a chance to get a reading on our position, but that wasn't going to be possible. I thought we were at the center of Ungava Bay.

We started out with our rations and an emergency kit, in our life raft that we were pulling like a sled. We set out in an easterly direction. We struggled over ice cliffs, and then through deep snow. Sometimes we were just in time to stare into a deep crevice. Night was falling. Bobby set to work building a snow hut. We felt better as we settled inside. For the first time, there was relief from the wind.

When we woke on the 19th of February, the morning was clear and crisp. We climbed to the top of one of the huge ice ridges. To the east we saw clouds that indicated open water. In the west, and from the direction we had come from the day before, we saw a high banking of clouds, and the contour of a skyline. We continued to travel to the east, but made little progress. On the 20th, there were high clouds again to the west. This meant there was land to the west and not to the east. We decided without much discussion to head back to the west. That was more or less the last clear view of the sky we had for the next four days because the weather closed in. We trudged on, hoping for the best. On one occasion, I thought we were on land, but I couldn't tell. That was before I heard Bobby call.

"Stop!"

"What's the matter?" asked Terry as he looked carefully around. We had taken to trudging against the ever-present wind with our heads down. We depended on Bobby to get us through.

"Water," he said. We stood at the edge of open water that was much too long to go around. We got into the raft and crossed to the other side.

At night I laid awake wandering if we would hear an airplane if it flew over. That wouldn't have mattered anyway. The bad weather would have kept any airplane from getting into the air for a search. We had to keep marching.

You lose your strength after a long enough trek in these conditions. You could also say that you lose a bit of your mind with your strength. That is what happened. It felt as if the trek would never end when we sat down one more time to rest.

"I say we should dump some of this," said Terry.

"We have to be careful about leaving anything behind."

"We just can't keep pulling the raft over drifts and cliffs like this anymore."

"It is tough."

Bobby stood quietly not saying anything.

"We take twice the effort to get over any obstacle. We could leave many of these extra clothes behind." There was little argument. I knew that we had to do something. "We have been getting closer to land all the time. We should make it soon." Soon, there was nothing left except the raft and rations. We decided to drop the raft and split the rations, but because there were more rations than we could pack, we left some of the food behind too.

We were desperate for any kind of sign that land was near, or even just in front of us. On the 24th, we saw land in the distance. This time it was unmistakable.

"We can make it in no time," said Terry.

"Maybe," I said.

Bobby watched carefully. I knew there was still a difficult trip in front of us. Bobby had been very quiet and steady as we went. I swear that he was the only one of us that knew where we were and where we had been. He was the only one to admit it to himself.

"If we can make it in one walk, we should do it," said Terry.

"It will be some time."

"I want to keep going until we make it, even if it takes all night and tomorrow."

"Our supplies are very low," I admitted.

"Yeah." said Bobby.

With that, we decided it was time to push ourselves. We couldn't stop now. Since we left the raft behind, we felt sick at the sight of another wide stretch of open water. There were many ice packs. Bobby found one large enough to hold us. That was risky business at the best of times because with men on a small ice flow, there is a chance that the weight will tip it at any moment. Submerging in Arctic water meant a quick death. Nevertheless, we mounted the ice and pushed off. It was the only chance we had. Soon, we jumped off the ice at the far side. I would swear that the ice we jumped from tipped and rolled over only a moment after we were safe.

We kept on. Without many stops, we trekked toward the land. After the food had run out, we were trekking on a prayer. We slumped down on the ice, feeling defeated. Bobby said that we shouldn't move for a while until he came back.

I thought the Inuit knew that we were finished and that our only chance was for him to try to find help to rescue us. I guess that was only another way of giving up. I sat back and thought about where we could be. Some time later, I heard crunching in the snow. I couldn't believe what I saw. There was Bobby pulling a walrus.

We eagerly ate the raw meat. I soon started to feel warm. We marched on through the night, but the next day we were still not on land. Finally, later that day, we reached the land. The three of us continued to move until the 28th when we met an Inuit with his wife and dog team. Bobby talked to them. They agreed to lead us to Port Burwell.

My worst fear was correct. The land we had reached was the Labrador coast. We had been out on the Atlantic ice for nine days. When I radioed the last message, I told the men in the survey station that I was in the center of the Ungava Bay. That was where they concentrated their search. They had flown hundreds of miles searching every chance they had. They flew 1,500 miles searching with the help of the RCMP, the Hudson's Bay Company, and the captain and crew of a steamer, the *Canadian Raider*. They thought we were dead by the time we arrived. The person who saved us was Bobby. The aircraft was never found. We never knew exactly where I came down.

After the work was done, when the old maps of the Hudson Straight were thrown out and new ones drawn up, the survey crew was able to supply some of the most important early information on the ice flows and the icebergs that helped many ships during the Second World War.

32. Saskatoon's First Lady Of the Sky

I guess I never told you the story about Nellie Irene Carson. I really should tell you that one. For most of us at the Saskatoon Aero Club, it was a bit of a surprise when she began flying. She was outgoing, but we didn't expect her to take flying lessons.

She joined us at the Saskatoon Aero Club in 1929. We all thought she had come for the thrill of flying. She was always going up with us. Sure, we said we were teaching her to fly, but we were amused when she took the controls for her dual lessons. We found out fast that she was good. The instructor told her to turn left and to turn right. She performed all the maneuvers well. The real test came when she had to correct the biplane from a spin.

In a spin, the nose is down and the world spins around you. It is one of the most disorienting sensations you could have in a biplane. You have to get the machine to go down faster first. You have to push the throttle forward all the way to get as much power out of the motor as you can. That gives you the power and "wind" so that the flaps will do what you want them too. The first time you do it, it feels like you're doing the opposite of what you should be doing. The natural reaction is to pull up and fly away. You want to slow the fall and pull the throttle back to a slow speed. Yet, if you don't have the power in the first place, you can't stop the spin and you can't pull up. You have to speed the motor up to full power and turn the flaps in the opposite direction of the spin to stop the spin. After that is done, you are in a simple dive, which you can pull up from.

Most students show how bold they are on this maneuver. Nellie wasn't scared at all when she first corrected for a spin.

Before we knew it, on September 30, 1929, Nellie was flying alone for her last test and she got her pilot's license.

The next summer, she was busy going to all the summer fairs across Saskatchewan. She could do all the stunts just like the rest of us: flying up side down, spins and low flying. Nellie was successful at giving rides as well. She charmed a lot of timid country boys (and the bold ones too) into going for a ride at three dollars apiece.

I remember on particular boy at a fair. He knew everything about everything.

"Looks easy," he said as he walked around Nellie's biplane. The music of the fair was loud. The breeze was warm. Children ran along the grass beside the aircraft.

"It is easy," said Nellie. She smiled as she looked at her machine.

"I'll bet I could take the controls and fly this machine right away."

"Well, you're bright and strong. Of course you could," she replied.

"All you have to do is pull, push and move that stick back and forth to turn, right?"

"That's right."

"Well, let's go. I'll show you."

"Sure," said Nellie.

Soon, the airplane was skipping down the runway. Nellie was in front and the boy was in the back. In the sky, the machine made a nice figure eight with the wings sloping each way, and then a simple right turn. When it was flat and wide, the boy had the controls. The plane spiraled higher and higher. In a moment, the airplane went into a spinning nosedive; I could see the rudder turn one way then the other. The boy was trying to correct the fall. Finally, the motor sped up and the flaps took control of the wind. The spinning stopped and the biplane pulled up. It made a wide loop and came into a landing.

"Good flying!" called Nellie as she jumped out of the plane. "You got your three dollars worth," she said. She walked with a high step to the concession in the fair grounds. She still hadn't come down from the excitement. Neither had the boy. I had to help him out of the plane. He tried to walk away calmly, but he was having trouble just standing.

Later that day, Nellie took her biplane up for her regular demonstration. She did all her usual stunts. At the time Nellie usually prepared to land, she began to climb. She went higher and higher. Her plane became smaller until we couldn't hear or see her. That day was June 8, 1930. That was the day she took her Moth biplane up to 16,000 feet, an altitude record for a woman.

Nellie joined the women's division of the Royal Canadian Air Force in 1942 and became a corporal. Soon, she was recommended for an officer's course at Toronto. I lost touch with her after that.

33. Saving Little Red River

Well, once the airplane was around, we pilots expected to supply air services when the need arose. That's why we didn't hesitate when we were asked to carry the antitoxin up north in the bitter cold of winter to save a community from an outbreak of diphtheria. The only other way to get the medicine there was to put it on a slow train to Peace River, then have a few dog teams run it out. The dogs would have taken over two weeks to do that kind of run. By the time the antitoxin arrived, it would have been frozen solid and useless.

We are Vic Horner, my partner and myself, "Wop" May. Our company was called the Commercial Airways of Alberta Ltd. The Little Red River was about 600 miles north of Edmonton. In the middle of December in 1929, there was an outbreak of diphtheria in that small community. The first victim was a

Hudson's Bay Company man who died from it. Many others became ill with it shortly after that.

On December 18th, a dog sled musher went to Fort Vermillion, around fifty miles away for help. There was a doctor there, but the small supply of antitoxin was too old to be useful. There was no equipment available to make any new antitoxin either. Fort Vermillion didn't have a telegraph. To send the message that the people of Little Red River needed help, the musher had to take the very long trail to Peace River where the railway ended and there was a telegraph. That was 300 miles away! He headed out, but didn't make it to Peace River until January 1, 1930. When he arrived, he had the telegraph sent to Edmonton.

Immediately after the message arrived in Edmonton, the Department of Health contacted our company. As soon as we heard the story, we didn't think twice about agreeing to fly the antitoxin to Fort Vermillion. The only plane available was our Avro Avian, a small machine with only a 75-horse power motor in it. The Avian had an open cockpit, which made flying uncomfortable, but I thought that if we dressed for the cold, we would make it. There was one more problem: we didn't have any skis for the biplane. That meant we had to land with our summer wheels, but we still thought that we could do it if we were very careful.

The Department of Health set to work. Soon, they had 600,000 units of antitoxin and something called toxoid, enough medicine to treat about 200 people with the disease. Because of the cold, they wrapped the medicine in woolen rugs and placed a charcoal heater inside the parcel to keep it from freezing. I asked if they might have an extra charcoal burner to put under my seat, but there was no answer. I guess the man who gave us the medical supplies was pretty serious. He was the Deputy Minister of Health, Dr. M. R. Bow. He also gave us a special tracheotomy set and an incubation set to loan to the northern village.

By the time we were ready to take off, it was 12:45 in the afternoon. Before that, I took one of the men aside to ask for a little help.

"I need some help."

"Sure."

"Go to the telegraph office. Send a message to McLennan Junction, that's about 265 miles north. Tell them we are coming. Ask them to clear a landing strip because we don't have skis."

"Okay. Should they clear off the road?"

"I don't know if there are roads up there. Ask them to clear some of the ice on the lake."

"All right."

As we flew north, I wasn't sure that we would make it to the Junction. The short winter day was coming to an end quickly. I felt much better after the Junction came into view. I circled once, saw the cleared area and landed safely.

The next morning we were up early, but there was no light to take off for some time. It was a typical winter day in the North. Finally, at 9:40, we had the Avro Avian running and skipping down the ice. Our next stop was Peace River, which was about fifty miles away. We landed at half past ten o'clock. We stayed on the ground just long enough to refuel. I was in a hurry to take off just in case there was a break down. If there was enough time, we could still make it before nightfall even if we had to do repairs. We were lucky. There were no problems as we lifted from the runway on our last jump to Fort Vermillion. At the same time, we had 280 miles to cover and there was very little daylight left.

The weather was cold. The flying was grueling. Engines often quit in such low temperatures, but that didn't happen. At 4:30 in the afternoon, we had only a few minutes left before dark. Then, in the whiteness of the snow, and the roughness of the bush, we spotted Fort Vermillion. We landed just in time. The sky was dark as we skidded to a stop.

No time was lost. A dog sled pulled up to the Avro as soon as we landed. The musher was ready to pick up the antitoxin and other supplies. He was soon loaded. He then disappeared into the bush to make the final trek to Little Red River. As light came up on the isolated community, the dog team came into view.

Even though we didn't admit it, we were both frost bitten. The next morning, we just wrapped ourselves up and then headed back to Edmonton, making a lot more stops along the way to warm up. When we arrived in Edmonton on the 6th of January, a huge crowd was waiting for us. It was strange because as we circled to land, it looked like we were coming into a summer fair, except the ground was covered with snow. There were many congratulations. The dog mushers who pushed through to Peace River and through the bush with the serum in the night were the real heroes, I thought.

34. The Bear Attack

My name is Walter Gilbert. Many folks ask me about this story. It's the one about the flight I made into central British Columbia to rescue a poor fellow who had a run-in with a grizzly. In September 1929, I was flying for Western Canada Airways in Vancouver. One day when I arrived at the aerodrome to start work, the owner quickly approached me.

"Morning," I said.

"We have a quick job we have to run for Consolidated Mining and Smelting," he said. I nodded, expecting a typical supply run.

"Where do I have to fly?"

"Burns Lake."

"That's way out," I said.

"Yes."

"What's so important that I have to fly there?"

"It's what you have to bring back that is important."

"Really?" Maybe there is a valuable *find* that I have to bring back?

"It's the Superintendent of the Emerald Mine. His name is H. C. Hughes."

"Oh, really?" I said. A big shot that wanted an easy ride out. I wasn't too fussy about flying such royalty.

"You'll have to bring his nurse along as well."

"Oh? Is he sick?"

"Injured pretty bad."

"Really?"

"He may be. From what I was told, he got between a grizzly and her cubs."

"Oh?"

"The company wants him flown out and brought to the hospital as fast as you can fly."

I had to get ready quickly. By early afternoon, I was flying out of Stewart. The flight was 260 miles. It seemed to take forever to get there, but it was only two hours and ten minutes before I was landing. Since it was too late to fly back to Vancouver that night, I stayed there. Early the next morning, I was ready to take the two to the city.

"How's he doing?" I asked the nurse. The superintendent looked terrible with all those bandages on. He was only muttering now and then. I couldn't believe it, but I actually thought that there were parts of his scalp missing.

"Time will tell," she said nervously.

"Don't worry about the flying."

"No," she said as the line on her forehead deepened. Maybe I shouldn't have said that.

"I'll try to fly as smoothly as I can, but you can never predict what kind of turbulence there will be."

"Oh?"

"Have you ever flown before?"

"No."

Again I bit my tongue.

Soon, we were lifting off from the lake. As we got up to altitude, the nurse began to relax. When we were over Quesnel, I began to lose altitude.

"What's the matter?" called the nurse from the back. "What are you doing?"

"Landing," I said. I guess I should have told her that there were stops.

"Why?"

"We need fuel."

"What? I thought we were just going to fly through to Vancouver."

"These machines can't fly that far on one tank of gasoline."

"We'll make it to Vancouver today, won't we?"

"Yes, we should. That is, if we have no break downs."

"What?"

"Hang on now, we're landing!"

When the pontoons set down on the water, the plane came to a fast stop. The nurse was more upset about the flying than the Superintendent.

It wasn't too long before we were in the air again. Soon, we had to land in Bridge River. I could see that the nurse was no happier with this landing than she had been with the first one. Like the first stop, we were fuelled up quickly and continued on our way again.

279

Finally, Vancouver came into sight.

"There's the city!" I called.

"Good," she said. She wasn't happy, but I had made the distance, about 520 air miles, in only six hours and forty minutes. I was satisfied with my progress.

An ambulance was standing by. The nurse hurried the attendants to get the Superintendent out of the aircraft and into the ambulance. I don't think that was strictly because of the man's condition.

I was right about the Superintendent. He had lost a good part of his scalp. Some time later, I heard that he had made a complete recovery.

35. Yukon Rescue

It was very dangerous to fly into the high north in 1930. I remember rescuing a couple of men who had trouble while they were flying in the Yukon. That was when I was asked to help. I'm Joe Walsh.

The story started when a prospector, Robert Martin, hired a commercial airplane, a Junker to be specific, with Paddy Burke as the pilot and Emile Kading as the flight engineer. On October 10, 1930, they were to fly from Atlin to Liard post, often called the Lower Post. The next day they were to fly back to Atlin. On their way back, they were supposed to follow a route over Teslin, Gladys, and then the Surprise Lakes. As usual for that region, a heavy snowstorm closed in on them not long after they took off and before they reached the mountains. They were flying blind. Paddy Burke turned the machine around and headed back to land on the Liard River before it became impossible to even do that. They made it down onto the river, made themselves comfortable and stayed the night.

It was snowing as heavily the next morning, but Paddy thought that if he got up there, he could get ahead of the bad weather. But, fortune had already turned against the crew. Only fifteen minutes after they took off, the weather got worse. Paddy turned around, and then made another landing on the Liard River. They came in for a landing well enough, but one of the pontoons of the Junker hit a rock in midstream and ripped open. Paddy quickly brought the machine to the shore.

The shore was one huge strip of deep mud. There was no way for the three men to drag the aircraft out of the water and no way for them to repair the pontoon if it was half submerged in heavy mud. They were not too worried about the situation because when Burke left Atlin, he told his wife that if they weren't back on time to contact the owners of the Junker in Vancouver, the Air Land Manufacturing Company, to arrange a rescue.

Now, in the northern bush in the Yukon, the winter gets so cold that a quick rescue is needed. When I think about my own flights in the high north, I have second thoughts now about what I did then. Since I always expected to be back soon, I never worried too much. That was a mistake. When you're that close to the Arctic Circle *worry*! When the men came for the gold in the Yukon Klondike in the 1890s, it was the law that they had to arrive with a year's supply of food, and ammunition. When we were flying in many

282

of the same latitudes, we carried supplies for only a couple of days.

Even though the Burke party expected to be rescued within a few days, they started rationing their food right away. Besides the shortage of food, the group was unprepared in other ways. Of the three sleeping bags they brought along, only one was heavy enough for winter conditions. Their rifle was a 30-30 with only twelve shells. They also had no cooking utensils. An old oil can was used to boil water.

Well, it didn't take Kading very long to start hunting. If he was going to have any success, he needed time. There were few animals around at that time of year. The group realized that the food, even if strictly rationed, would not last long enough.

After a week, the men decided they had to move on. One plan was to take the hundred feet of rope they had, build a raft and float down stream to the nearest settlement, which was quite far away. There were problems with that idea. Only Kading could swim. Also, if they had to go any distance at all, the rocky river would rip up the ropes before they arrived anywhere.

The Burke party had a large cache of food at Junkers Lake from the summer before. Their second plan was to head for the lake on foot, leaving a note behind on a tree to say where they went. Now that sounds like a good idea, but in knee-deep snow with no snowshoes, it is a little crazy. Added to that, the men were wearing light flying boots. They had no winter gear. They expected to get the food, and then go on to Wolf where there was a winter camp of natives. With this hope in mind, they set out on October 17th with their remaining food, their precious oilcan, rifle, and sleeping bags.

As planned, Mrs. Burke contacted the company in Vancouver as soon as he husband did not arrive on schedule. Some time passed before they made arrangements with the pilot R. I. Van der Byl, W. A. Jorass, and T. H. Cressy. From what I understand, they ran into trouble up at Thutade Lake, north of Hazelton in British Columbia. After that, the Vancouver Company contacted the Tredwell, Yukon Company, based in White Horse, to look for the lost crew. The Yukon Company put together a crew with a pilot from International Airways who stopped in town during a flight from Seattle, Washington to Cordova, Alaska. He began flights out of Atlin on October 26th. However, the Yukon Company had also agreed to fly a number of prospectors out of their summer camps before winter. This is what the pilot now had to turn his attention to.

The White Horse Company enlisted the services of another pilot, Everett L. Wasson, to fly a number of risky flights in November and December.

At the same time, a prospector who had heard about the lost men arrived in Vancouver. The prospector was Sam Clerf, a good friend of Burke and Martin. He interrupted his trip to San Francisco, where his wife waited with a newborn son, to charter an airplane from Alaska Airways, with Pat Renahan as the pilot and Frank Hatcher as the engineer, to rescue his friends. The flight went well until they reached Butedal, on the British Columbia coast, on November

4th. They intended to fly across to Prince Rupert and then head north, but a thick fog came up fast. The aircraft never made it to Prince Rupert. That brought about a search by the Royal Canadian Air Force. After a long search, only a single tire that had washed up on a small coastal island was found.

The search that was organized earlier by the Tredwell Company continued throughout this time. When the pilot Wasson flew over the Liard Post, he couldn't land because he was still equipped with pontoons, which are not suitable for landing on snow and ice. The aircraft circled Laird while the pilot wrote a note asking if Burke had traveled through earlier. The reply was to be written in the snow. It was "Yes," but the message also said that the men had set out for Teslin on October 11th. Even though the man below wrote out the name Teslin twice in the snow, he must have meant to write Atlin. The pilot thought Burke might have gone there because it was his habit to visit Teslin on his final trip home for the winter. That mistake meant that hundreds of miles in a dangerous, unmapped region of the Yukon were needlessly searched.

With much of the open water freezing over, Wasson decided to head back to Mayo to have the pontoons replaced with skis. That is where he met me and told me the story of the search. Since I had a lot of experience as a guide in the area, I agreed to go along.

* * *

The four lost men made about four miles in their first day they set out. They continued like this for about a week until Burke was completely exhausted, then they set up camp. It was October 24th when the three men sat down to eat the last of their food. From that day until November 15th, all they had to eat was a duck and four small squirrels. The hunting Kading did was limited to an area very close to their camp. He found no tracks and didn't hear any sounds. On November 15th, the men spotted a caribou about two hundred feet from their camp. With a lot of luck, Kading was able to bring the animal down with one shot. Martin and Kading worked quickly to get the meat and to make soup for Burke, who looked very weak, but the food came too late. Burke died on November 20th.

The other two men buried Paddy in a sleeping bag, marking the spot by hanging his boots on the tree over the grave. Then, they packed up as much meat as they could carry and moved on again. Their environment hadn't changed and neither had their progress through the snow. After a day of walking, more like struggling, they had moved five miles. They sat down, totally exhausted. All they could do was set up camp and keep a fire going. The real loss, I would say, was that during the time up until that day, they hadn't heard an airplane. On the trail, they listened helplessly as one flew over then disappeared in the distance. The men couldn't even send a message with fire because there was no time to build one. To save their energy, the two made a habit of staying in their sleeping bags from 2:00 o'clock in the afternoon until 8:00 o'clock in the morning. With the frostbite they had, that was the best decision they could have made.

* * *

The pilot, Wasson and myself had to wait for the new skis for our aircraft to arrive from White Horse. That was on November 12th. I remember Wasson telling me about the search he had been doing until then.

"Well, after we got that sign from Liard Post, we spent our time looking in the region between Liard Post and Teslin," said Wasson.

"Did you ever fly straight through from Liard Post to Atlin?" I asked.

"No."

"It seems we should start looking in that area right away."

"That is rough country through there."

"I know that."

"The peaks in that region are between five and seven thousand feet high. At least, that is what I had figured them to be when I flew over them."

"A hard trek on foot."

"Impossible. Are there any maps of that area at all?"

"None. I don't know how a map could be made."

"We'll have to be careful all right."

"The real problem is going to be the weather. If there isn't a snow squall, that means there is one about to begin."

"Don't remind me of that."

Well, we agreed to search the region between the Liard Post and Atlin. We set off on November 12th. It took some searching before we even got close to where Burke's Junkers came down. We had a breakthrough when we landed at the mouth of the Liard. A group of natives we met there told us that a large swan had flown over.

We kept looking, but the severe snowstorms were continuous. At times, a storm closed in every hour. When we were lucky enough to take off, we searched intensely for a few minutes before the snow would start falling again, forcing us to drop down onto another lake. I remember one time, when we were on a small lake; it took ten runs before we got into the air. Often, we had to pack a snow runway just to take off. The one take off that I remember most was when we had tried everything we could think of, but the sticky snow was holding the aircraft back. We decided that I would hold onto the door and push the machine just to get some speed up. It worked, but the airplane seemed to jump off the snow a bit. I was hanging on with all my strength when my shoes were grabbed by the wind. I made it into the cabin with a lot of luck.

Finally, we caught a glimpse of what seemed like a strange shadow on the Liard. We flew in close to look at it. It was the missing Junker. We flew back to White Horse for more equipment and supplies, and then flew back again. We searched the area for a place to land, but the river was covered with huge drifts and ice piles. The closest place we could find was a small lake sixteen miles away. We trekked to the spot. After we found the message that the men had gone upstream, we struggled back to our plane, and flew back to White Horse. There we talked and decided that there was a chance that the men had made their way to the Pelly Reserve. We were heading back and on December 6th, searching for a way to fly through the Pelly Range of mountains, when we saw a string of smoke floating up from the tree coverage below. Wasson flew in closer. There were two dark images that looked like men waving their hands at us.

"There they are!" called Wasson.

"Looks like it."

"They're going to need some food."

"No doubt about that."

"I'll fly in close. You open the door and kick out the box of food when I tell you to. Put a note in the box saying we are going to land right away."

"Okay," I said as I grabbed the box of emergency food. I wrote the note, put it inside the box and was barely ready when he yelled "Now!" I kicked the box out, and then quickly closed the door.

"Damn, that was off too far, I think. Those men aren't going to be able to get to it. We'll have to throw the other box right in the camp area," I said.

"That's our food."

"Yeah, I know."

"All right."

I grabbed the next box. Wasson flew in low, just above the treetops. He yelled again. Out went the second box.

"That one was good. We'll have to find a place to land," said Wasson.

"I agreed. We need our grub back."

Well it wasn't too long before we saw a lake to land on. It was ten miles away. As night was coming in quickly, we rushed out of the aircraft with our snowshoes. We were almost running, but there wasn't enough time. We had to *siwash*; that means we were stopped by the darkness before we could make a camp. We just waited for the morning. Neither of us slept very well. Before dawn, we were on our way again. We were moving fast, when I realized that we had gone to far. We turned back, yelling their names as we went. Then, we heard two shots of a rifle. That was all it took to set us on our way right to their camp.

When we found the two in the bush, they looked pathetic, frost bitten and thin. Yet, they were able to find both boxes of food and eat. We helped ourselves to some of the food too.

Because we expected the men to have at least one pair of snowshoes, we just brought along one extra set. I had to hack down some branches to make a pair of old fashioned ones for Kading so that we could get them back to the plane. Finally, on December 10th, we made it. It was early enough in the day to get the motor going. That was not an easy task after the plane had been sitting a long time in the wind and cold, but we were lucky enough to get it started. We made it back to White Horse that day.

Later, Wasson, Sergeant Leopold of the Royal Canadian Mounted Police and myself flew back into the bush, found Burke's body and brought it back for a proper burial.

In the investigation that followed, no blame was laid for Burke's death. It was decided that airmen had to carry more safety equipment and more food if they wanted to fly in the Yukon. That made sense to me. As a guide in those regions, I still believed that only the lucky ones make it back.

36. A Boy Scout in the Sky

Yes, I knew Pat, who was Kirkpatrick Maclure
Sclanders, the kid who could fly. We all called him
Pat. I don't know if he was really a Boy Scout, but he
was dressed up like one the day he jumped into the
cockpit of an idling biplane at the summer fair in front
of all those people and accidentally took off. Well, that
was something; everyone watched silently, completely
shocked. The dumb kid was going to kill himself.

I'll have to go back to the beginning to tell you the
whole story. To start with, Pat was from Saskatoon,
Saskatchewan, but he ended up here in St. John, New
Brunswick. He was a teenager when I first saw him
around the St. John Flying Club asking questions,
begging for rides, and doing errands for us. We didn't
think much of it. We just thought that he would be a
member of the club some day. Except, when he was
fifteen, he entered a contest sponsored in the United
States. He had to read an article on aviation and flying,

293

then write out all the errors in it. The contestant who found the most errors won. You really had to know lots of details about flying to win a contest like that. That was something, but that kind of knowledge didn't always make you a pilot. You also had to have some skill and coordination in flying to be a pilot.

We found out soon after that how much commitment Pat had to flying. He was only fifteen, as he would point out, when he joined the flying club. There was only one reason to join the club: to learn how to fly. That is exactly what Pat set out to do when he signed up for lessons. He went up for his first dual lesson on August 18th, 1931.

I was the instructor. My name is Clifford Kent. The lessons were given in a standard De Havilland Moth. As soon as we were up, I let Pat take the controls. He set to flying the machine. We went from side to side, then up and down, as if he we checking out whether I had really let go of the stick and the foot peddles. He continued to fly wide circles. I thought that was pretty good for a kid that young.

Now I learned a long time ago that flying wasn't the mathematics, the meteorology or the aerodynamics. Flying is knowing the feel of the machine and the wind and reacting to it as if you were a part of the plane. As far as I'm concerned that means that the younger ones who set out to learn to fly are more likely to learn faster. They never stop to think about what they were told on the ground. Instead, the young flyers will take the biplane up and fly until they know what everything feels like. That is what happened with Pat. He caught on fast. I could see that he had a feel for it.

The day came when I really wanted to know if this kid could take the hardest pulls the biplane could offer. I took Pat up and told him to take the controls for a while, and then I told him I was taking the control. As the airplane gained altitude, I pulled the machine up hard enough to stall it. The machine headed downward in a full spin. Pat easily brought the motor up to full throttle, corrected the spin and pulled up. I introduced a hard push on the stick so that the aircraft would tumble, but Pat's reactions were fast and correct. I continued to test Pat, but nothing bothered him. As a matter of fact, I would have to say that he enjoyed it. When I told him to bring the machine down, he protested that the lesson had been too short. After we landed, I jumped out of the cockpit. As usual, Pat sat there; not wanting to believe it was over for another day.

"Well, you stay there, Pat."

"The motor is still running," he said, inquiring if he should switch it off.

"That's right, I need a coffee break. Why don't you finish this lesson without me?"

"Sure!"

"Don't get carried away. Remember how much fuel we have already used."

"Yeah, I know. Time goes by twice as fast up there."

"Well, hurry up. I have another lesson."

With that, I heard the motor speed up. The Moth was skipping down the runway in a moment. I did what I said I was going to do. I went into the hangar for a coffee break. As far as I was concerned, Pat was a qualified pilot.

That solo flight was on August 18, 1931. That made Pat the youngest person in Canada to make a solo flight. By the end of that year, he had flown eleven hours and five minutes. He would have flown much more if we had given him the chance. He just kept flying even though he was too young to get his pilot's license. In those days, you could fly without a license, but you couldn't take a passenger with you.

Well, at the summer fair in Charlotte Town, our flying club was putting on a show. I was the pilot who demonstrated some of the skills for the bystanders. At the end of that particular show, I landed the Moth on the racing track in front of the crowd. I jumped out of the cockpit, then the man on the loud speaker said, "Now it is important that you stay away from the aircraft when it is running. We wouldn't want any accidents."

After this announcement was made, Pat stepped out of the crowd in a boy scout uniform, which made him look much younger than he already looked. He was one of those boys who looked very young at sixteen. I would say he looked like he was eleven or twelve. He stepped up to the biplane and looked at the flaps for a moment as the crowd started to take notice. In a very short time, he was climbing onto the wing and into the cockpit. People were really getting worried. To them, it looked like he was looking around the cockpit, but he was really strapping himself in for the flight. As the engine roared, I came out from behind the grandstand yelling, "STOP!"

I swear that there were about five mothers on their way out to the racetrack. They probably thought they knew the boy roaring down the strip. The crowd was on its feet yelling and talking. The Master of Ceremonies was telling them to please sit down. I thought for a minute that the women making their way down the steps would come after me for letting it happen. By this time, the Moth was swerving as it picked up speed down the runway. At the last moment, the plane straightened out and climbed into the air. The crowd became silent. To my relief, the mothers stopped and stared like the rest. Pat didn't fool around. He went to a good height, and then stalled. The machine spun downward. It was during the moment of suspense that the announcer broke the silence:

"Word has reached me that we are now watching the demonstration of a fully trained pilot, Pat Sclanders of the St. John Flying Club."

To prove the point, the biplane stopped its spin, and then pulled up. The crowd didn't believe what happened at first, but as the aircraft above them looped and spun again. Slowly, they sat down. The crowd began to whisper to each other. Now, that was a show that few forgot.

Pat's seventeenth birthday was on January 2, 1933. He took his pilot's test and received his license. The bad weather that year prevented Pat from taking up his first passenger until the 19th. By the end of 1934, he had 50 hours and 30 minutes of flying time. That's when he had to give up flying for a job.

He must have been thinking of flying every day he was working. At the end of 1936, he thought of a way of flying every day. He bought a ticket to England where he enlisted in the Royal Air Force. He had to go to England to join the air force because in the middle of the Great Depression, the Canadian government was not accepting any new pilots into the military. Even the best men from Mount Royal College had to go to England to get a commission.

Pat became a Flight Lieutenant, but he was released from his duties because of an illness. When the war started in 1939, Pat applied to the RCAF, but was rejected because of his earlier illness.

That didn't stop Pat, though. He joined some American pilots who wanted to enter the war. Together, they were on their way to Finland to fly for the Finnish army, but it was too late. The Germans had already invaded.

The men went to Paris where they enlisted with the French Air Force, but the German forces invaded. The pilots had to flee across country staying just out of the way of the invading German army for a couple of weeks. They finally got to a port on the channel, slipped across to England, and hurried to the recruitment offices of the Royal Air Force. Their timing was just right. England had to create a massive air force over night. All the pilots were immediately enlisted. They took part in the Battle of Britain.

The story is that Pat was in the group that was scrambled to take on a massive German attack. Pat's group had only ten airplanes. They flew out over the channel to face a formation of 110 German aircraft. That was his last fight.

I have many memories of Pat, but the event that I remember the most vividly was that day when I jumped out of my Moth and he jumped in and the way the crowd reacted when they thought they were about to witness a tragic accident.

About the Author

Peter Conrad brings his interest in aviation history and his skills as a storyteller together in *First Flights*. Peter published *Training for Victory: the British Commonwealth Air Training Plan in the West* with Douglas and McIntyre. He has also published various historical articles, short stories, and the young adult novel, *Other Choices*.

Printed in the United States
15622LVS00001B/48

9 781414 046020